# THE SILENT WARRIORS

# *THE* SILENT WARRIORS

## by Joshua Tadmor

☙ ☙ ☙

TRANSLATED FROM THE HEBREW BY

## Raphael Rothstein

*THE MACMILLAN COMPANY*

For

ELIE WEISEL,

without whose encouragement

this book would not have been written

# ❦ Contents

# ❦ Preface

FOR SEVERAL YEARS PRECEDING THE ESTABLISHMENT OF
the state of Israel, I worked for Israeli intelligence. I was
directly involved in activities concerning the Middle East and
indirectly acquainted with operations in other areas. Since
those days I have never stopped admiring many of the people
I encountered during that period.

They carried out many kinds of assignments, some more
dangerous than others. These men and women were always
taken far away from their homes and had to undergo periods
of isolation and loneliness while they kept their secrets and
heavy responsibilities to themselves. It often seemed a heavy
burden to me—more than the average person could bear.

But these were not average people and they were few in
number. Their daring, courage, and dedication knew no
limits. It was they who gave Israel the crucial strategic advantage that made it possible for the Jews to withstand the
overwhelming hostility and numerical superiority of the
Arab enemies surrounding them.

Some of the personalities depicted in this book are drawn
from a long list of anonymous men and women whose stories
have never been told in full. Following the Six Day War of
June, 1967, the curtain of secrecy was lifted slightly, but the
subsequent unrest in the Middle East has prevented full-
scale disclosures. As a result, most of the "silent warriors"
remain nameless.

9

The chapters of this book recount actual events and deeds that have been fully authenticated. However, Israel's security regulations presented certain difficulties. In the chapter entitled "The *Lino*," I omitted mention of several names in order to protect certain Italians who performed important services for Israel and who still hold official positions in Italy's naval administration. In this case these men appear under the collective name Bianco.

The events surrounding the *Lino* and *Brigand* episodes were familiar to me from the time I served in Italy. In addition, I was aided by letters and documents contained in the Haganah archives in Tel Aviv and by conversations with Yehuda Arzi, Munya Mardor, Amnon Yona, and many others who took part in the sea adventures.

In gathering material for the chapter on Yolande, I interviewed most of the people who worked in Cairo prior to 1948. These included Levi Avrahami, Yaacov Tsur, Eliahu Sassoon, and others. I also knew Yolande Hermor personally.

In preparing the above-mentioned chapters as well as other sections of this book I was helped by both present and former members of the Israel Intelligence Services. I wish to thank these dedicated people. They are in no way responsible for the final form of this book.

I have also made extensive use of the following sources: Dan Ben-Porat and Uri Yishiyahu, *HaMeragal She Ba Me-Yisrael*, Ramat Gan, 1968; Munya Mardor, *Ruah Gadola Baa;* Shmuel Segev, *Sadin Adom;* Haganah archives; Zionist archives; Israeli newspapers—*LaMerhav, Ha'aretz, Maariv, Yeditoh Ahronoth;* Israel Defense Forces publications; interviews with representatives of the Haganah and the Jewish Agency assigned to Egypt from 1944–1946; conversations and interviews with members of the Haganah and Israel Intelligence Services assigned to Italy from 1947 to 1950; continual contacts with Israeli security and intelligence personnel.

My special thanks to Raphael Rothstein who translated and edited this edition. His efforts and contribution exceeded those of a mere translator and editor.

JOSHUA TADMOR
Jerusalem

PART I

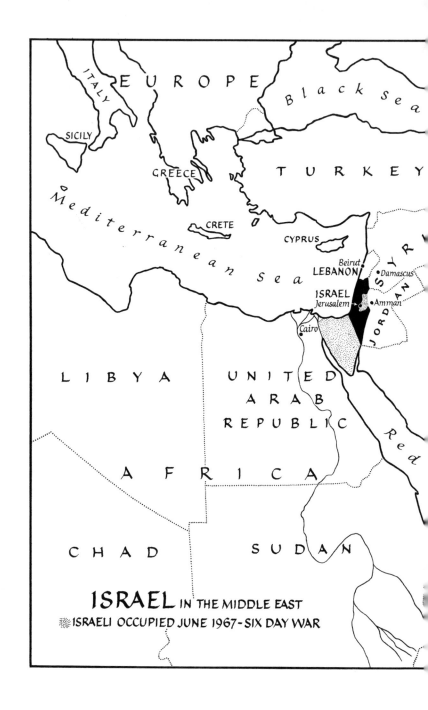

**ISRAEL** IN THE MIDDLE EAST
ISRAELI OCCUPIED JUNE 1967 – SIX DAY WAR

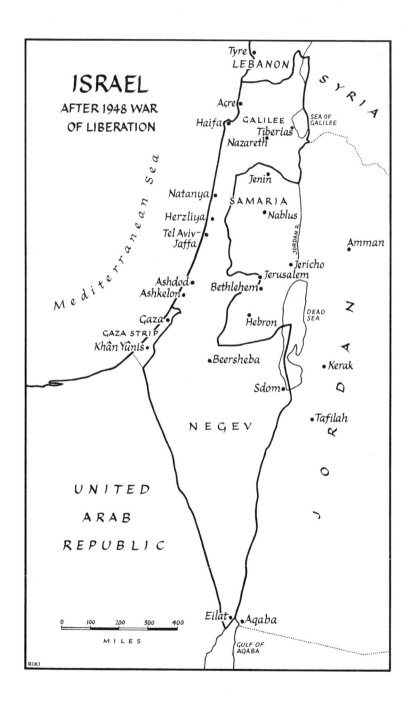

ISRAEL
AFTER 1948 WAR
OF LIBERATION

Mediterranean Sea

Tyre
LEBANON
SYRIA
Acre
Haifa
GALILEE
SEA OF
GALILEE
Tiberias
Nazareth
Jenin
Natanya
SAMARIA
Herzliya
Nablus
Tel Aviv
Jaffa
JORDAN R.
Amman
Jericho
Jerusalem
Ashdod
Bethlehem
Ashkelon
Gaza
Hebron
DEAD
SEA
GAZA STRIP
Khân Yûnis
JORDAN
Beersheba
Kerak
Sdom
Tafilah
NEGEV

UNITED

ARAB

REPUBLIC

0   100   200   300   400

MILES

Eilat   Aqaba
GULF OF
AQABA

RIKI

# ⚜ The Fight for Statehood

ON THE TWENTY-NINTH OF NOVEMBER, 1947, A fateful decision was made by the United Nations General Assembly. By a vote of thirty-three to thirteen it decided to end the British World War I mandate and partition Palestine into Jewish and Arab states with an international sector that would include Jerusalem, Lydda Airport, and other areas.

It was exactly midnight when the news reached Tel Aviv. It spread quickly throughout the country, giving relief to the tension that had built up over the U.N. vote. Everywhere people celebrated. Many, overwhelmed by emotion, ran into the streets crying. Elderly, bearded men hurried to synagogues to pray for peace and give thanks.

Every detail was widely discussed: How were the various representatives instructed by their governments? How did each country vote? Many talked of how Israel's representatives had struggled behind the scenes to secure votes in favor of partition.

People sought to savor the moment. In Dizengoff Circle in the center of Tel Aviv, in Zion Square and at the gates of the Jewish Agency in Jerusalem crowds began to gather. Tens of thousands of young people dressed in khaki shirts and shorts, many of them carrying guns, gathered in the main streets and centers of every city, village, and settlement in Israel. Their mood was ecstatic. Everywhere hands joined in dancing the Hora; songs of celebration and triumph echoed through the night.

A Jewish state! The vision of generations was realized after thousands of years of prayer and yearning. The vow, "If I forget thee, O Jerusalem," had been honored during centuries marked by persecutions, expulsions, pogroms, and genocide.

Veterans of the Zionist movement, those who had been involved from the days of Herzl and the Balfour Declaration, wept. The believers among them recited the appropriate blessing. These were the men who had tried to save their people from the Nazi holocaust, who had heard stories of the atrocities and death camps and were incredulous, the men who were empowered to grant the few permits issued for emigration to Palestine under the British mandate and whose terrible duty it was to choose those who would live. These were the leaders, who at the war's end saw the liberated concentration camps and the horrors wrought by the Germans and had to entreat the British to allow the hundreds of thousands of survivors—the children, the mothers, and the elderly, the broken and brutalized who sought nothing more than a chance to live and hope once again—to emigrate to Palestine.

But the British had refused and were unyielding. They would not be moved, and many young Jews went underground to oppose Foreign Minister Ernest Bevin's inhumane policy. The result was a small-scale war, one of terrorist acts and persistent sabotage. But it was an ugly war and many fell. It shocked world opinion and provoked fresh memories of the concentration camps and the fate of the Jews of Poland, Hungary, France, and Holland.

In defiance of the British blockade, boatloads of refugees sailed from Mediterranean ports after the war and some miraculously succeeded in eluding British naval patrols. They landed on Israel's shores at night and were proudly called the "illegals," for they had defied His Majesty's government's ban on immigration.

And then came international recognition of the Jews' right to their own country, a nation that would guarantee the right of every Jew to seek and find refuge among his brethren, a nation governed and defended by Jews. Refugees would arrive in daylight with the flag of Israel waving from ships' masts.

It would have been difficult for a non-Jew to understand the feverish dances and the joyous singing that swept Israel that night. Perhaps only one whose people had been denied freedom for thousands of years and then had struggled to regain it could appreciate the happiness that enveloped the Jewish nation on November 29, 1947.

But the celebrations were short-lived. The Arabs' threats to resist the formation of a Jewish state had not been empty. Those who opposed the U.N. decision sought to alter it by force of arms. Scattered incidents that had resembled the guerrilla and terrorist tactics of the anti-Jewish actions of 1929 and 1936–39 quickly assumed the dimensions of full-scale hostilities. Amin El Husseini, the Mufti of Jerusalem and the religious leader of Palestine's Moslem Arabs, sought to assure the intervention of the regular armies belonging to the Arab countries surrounding Palestine.

Israel, however, was skeptical of the possibility that her Arab neighbors would openly intervene on behalf of Palestine's Arab community. Those familiar with the Middle East claimed that insofar as the Arabs are concerned there is a considerable gap between word and deed and the threat of war did not necessarily mean war.

The Mufti also knew this. He was anxious to avoid the defeat of his irregular Arab fighters, should they be forced to fight the Jews without outside help. In accordance with this, he worked to aggravate the situation in Palestine in as rapid a fashion as possible. He was convinced that while the warlike declarations of the national leaders of the Arab nations were still fresh in the memory of their people, those leaders would be unable to avoid intervention once a conflict began.

The Mufti's plan was to launch a massive terrorist campaign and kill as many Jews as possible. He was sure that the Jewish Haganah and the Irgun fighting units would retaliate and the Arab nations would then be forced to come to the aid of their Palestinian brothers under attack. Thus the regular Arab armies would be openly committed to a war against the Jews.

Within a week after the U.N. partition vote, the Arabs of Palestine, incited by the Mufti, rose up in arms, and the bitterly contested land was plunged into civil war. The Mufti, in the name of the Supreme Arab Council, called a general strike. Stores were closed—some merchants were fr  ed to comply—work in factories and workshops ceased, schools were locked, and Arab transportation stopped. A hostile Arab mob converged on Jerusalem's business center, where there were both Jewish and Arab shops, and systematically smashed, looted, and burned the stores and beat up any Jews found in the streets.

As the war developed, the Jewish community got the worst of it. The Haganah at first acted with restraint and avoided embarking on reprisal actions in a vain effort to stem the increase of violence. Arab marauders threatened Tel Aviv, Haifa, Safed, and Tiberias. The road to Jerusalem was unsafe for Jewish travelers, and Arab snipers took a heavy toll. It was an easy matter for the Arabs to cut off remote Jewish settlements. Hundreds of Arab villages lined the roads leading to Tel Aviv, Haifa, Jerusalem, and the towns of Galilee, but many Jewish kibbutzim were isolated and widely scattered throughout the country.

"No retreat!" "Do not abandon any settlement!" These orders were sent to every Jewish point on the map. Lines of supply and communication were maintained by lightly armed convoys that faced Arab ambushes waiting on the sides of the roads and in the mountains.

The United Nations was unable to enforce its own resolution despite Secretary General Trygve Lie's efforts to pressure the United States and Great Britain into decisive action aimed at implementing the partition plan. Washington vacillated and had second thoughts about the partition scheme. The United States refused to supply the desperate Jews with arms and asked Britain to stay on in Palestine. The British, however, continued to withdraw and systematically handed over their army bases to the Arabs while hampering Jewish self-defense efforts. Both the United States and Britain shared the view that the tiny Jewish population of 650,000 shortly would be driven into the sea by the overwhelming numbers of regular Arab troops and irregulars.

The Haganah, faced with no choice, decided to go on the offensive, attacking Arab lines of transport and supply. Bridges were blown up and roads were mined, but such actions had little effect on the Palestinian Arabs who, because of their basically rural character, were able to get along without motorized transportation.

In the first round the Arabs had the advantage. The Jews suffered heavy losses, but somehow Jewish settlements and urban centers were able to hold on despite the severe lack of arms and the continual Arab siege. But this was only the beginning. David Ben-Gurion and the other Jewish leaders knew from Haganah intelligence reports that a massive Arab invasion was imminent. These reports were based on observation of the mobilization activities taking place in Arab countries and the tone of Arab press and radio propaganda.

The Haganah drew up a master plan calling for a strategic advance to control the areas granted to the Jewish state under the U.N. partition plan. As the British withdrew, the Jews had more freedom of movement, and the Haganah embarked on an intensive recruitment and training program in settlements and urban areas. Overnight, Haganah squads became companies and regiments. The underground fighting organization took on the dimensions of a regular army. But there was still a severe scarcity of arms and ammunition, and many units did not have enough rifles to go around.

The second round of the conflict began with the Jewish campaign to lift the siege of Jerusalem. Surrounded on three sides by Jordan, Jerusalem was under heavy bombardment by the Arab Legion, Jordan's British-trained and equipped army. The narrow, winding road from the coast through the Judean Hills was lined with Palestinian Arabs ready to attack any Jewish convoy making its way through the hills with food and water for the beleaguered Jewish sector of the city. The situation grew worse by the hour, and there seemed little hope that the city could hold out. It was short of food and water, and the Arab bombardment from the surrounding hills was relentless. But just when the struggle for Jerusalem seemed hopeless, several planes carrying machine guns and rifles from Czechoslovakia managed to land at an abandonded British installation where a crude and makeshift landing strip, illuminated by flashlights, had been fashioned. Quickly the heavy layer of grease covering the arms was scraped off, and the arms were loaded onto trucks and taken to Kibbutz Hulda in the Judean Hills. There the rifles were hastily distributed to the eager young members of the Haganah and its commando corps, the Palmach, and they set off to guard the convoys.

In the north, Haganah units drove back the Syrian "liberation army," an advance force of Arab volunteers sent to destroy Jewish settlements in the Jezreel Valley and cut Haifa off from Tel Aviv.

The clandestine shipment of arms from Czechoslovakia was made in defiance of an American-British arms embargo on the Middle East that seemed to apply solely to the Jews. The Palestinian Arabs were well supplied by neighboring Arab countries and the departing British army. Though the Jewish forces were ill equipped throughout the War of Liberation, those arms that did find their way into the hands of the Jews arrived in Israel thanks to the effort of a small, dedicated group of Haganah undercover agents operating in Europe with one aim and purpose: to provide Israel's defenders with everything needed to resist the Arabs and assure the survivial of the Jewish nation, whether it be secret arms purchases, recruitment of flyers, intelligence-gathering, or sabotage. These men and women fought the "silent war," the behind-the-scenes struggles for the establishment of the state of Israel, about which little is known to this day.

On May 14, 1948, David Ben-Gurion proclaimed Israel's existence as a sovereign state. Within twenty-four hours the armies of Iraq, Jordan, Syria, Lebanon, and Egypt invaded Palestine and joined the indigenous Arab troops in what they throught would be the total destruction of the Jews.

They were opposed by a tiny Jewish army of 35,000 men and women, many of them inexperienced and untrained new immigrants. Against the tanks, heavy artillery, and air power of the Arabs this Jewish force was equipped with 22,000 rifles—the majority of them secondhand—11,000 machine guns, 1,500 automatic rifles, 700 small mortars, 75 antitank weapons and four light cannons. Israel's miraculous victory was due to the indomitable spirit and courage of a young nation with no choice but to fight for its survival or face annihilation.

Every man, woman, and child was a soldier in a war that enveloped the entire nation. On May 26, 1948, the Haganah, its Palmach commando corps, the Irgun (fighting arm of the Revisionist Zionists), and the terrorist LEHI or Freedom Fighters of Israel (also known as the Stern Gang) were merged into the Israel Defense Forces which was organized into three commands—land, air, and sea.

Aided by the overconfidence, dissension, bad strategic planning, and low morale evident in the Arab forces, the Israeli army was able at great cost successfully to resist and finally rout the invaders. Heroic acts and uncommon sacrifice were displayed by Jewish soldiers and civilians in the face of superior Arab fire power. Many border kibbutzim turned back advancing columns of Arab tanks with nothing but a few rifles and Molotov cocktails.

To end the war which raged throughout 1948, the United Nations sent Count Folke Bernadotte of Sweden as a mediator, but after arranging a series of cease-fires he was assassinated by a Jewish terrorist in Jerusalem in September. Then Dr. Ralph Bunche sought to negotiate an armistice under U.N. auspices. But the fighting continued, with the Arabs suffering defeat after defeat.

In early 1949 the great powers pressured the warring parties to negotiate a settlement. Representatives of Israel and the Arab countries, with the exception of Iraq, which refused to participate in peace talks, met on the island of Rhodes and negotiated general armistice agreements recognizing *de facto* Jewish control over considerably more territory than had been allocated to a Jewish state under the original U.N. partition plan. Israel withdrew from Lebanese- and Egyptian-held territory. Syria and Jordan retreated in some sectors, but Jordan annexed the West Bank of Palestine in violation of the U.N. plan, which called for the establishment of a Palestinian Arab state in that area.

Already in 1947, Jewish agents on secret missions were active in many European cities and ports as well as in America and Canada, raising funds for the Zionist cause and keeping an eye on Arab international activity.

One important clandestine activity of Israeli agents occurred during the first truce period of the War of Liberation. On June 11, 1948, Count Bernadotte arranged a temporary one-month truce between Israel and the Arab armies. The respite enabled Israeli forces to consolidate the reorganization they had undergone in battle when the underground organizations merged into a regular army. This army could now integrate several mechanized units into its ground infantry brigades and steel itself for a counteroffensive. The U.N. stipulated, however, that during the truce the combatants would not be allowed to increase their strength by bringing in additional arms from the outside.

The Arabs were quick to disregard this and other provisions of the truce and made frenzied efforts to purchase arms and equipment for their armies. Preventing the arrival of as many of these shipments as possible while at the same time procuring crucial arms for the Israeli army was a major task of Israeli secret agents. They had few qualms about exploiting the U.N. truce in this respect because their very survival depended upon it.

Israel's leaders had long been aware of the significance of clandestine observation and assiduously applied long-range espionage endeavors.

In the years prior to the Arab invasion of 1948, Zionist leaders were concerned with developments in Egypt where the British sought to retain colonial control of a restless nation by meddling in the political conspiracies and plots played out by a dependent, corrupt monarch and the self-serving, ideologically bankrupt Wafd party. The nation, whose internal problems were intensified by World War II when it became the center of Allied operations in the region, was torn by political strife, social inequality, and the stirrings of a variety of several Arab nationalist causes.

Here to Palestine's south was the most culturally advanced of all Arab states seething with the agitations of extremist ideologies—right-wing Moslem fanatics, pan-Arabists, Communists, and pro-Axis Fascists. Further complicating the unhappy complexity of Egypt were the sizable ethnic and religious minorities—Jews, Copts, Greeks, and Italians—each community with its own language, customs, and spheres of economic interest. The major cities of such a heterogeneous, volatile nation were indispensable listening posts to any nation or interest group seeking to predict the shape of things to come in the Middle East.

The men dedicated to the founding of an independent Jewish state in Palestine placed a high priority on knowing what was happening behind the scenes in Cairo and Alexandria. Indeed, as history was to demonstrate, this special knowledge and the many unknown agents who provided it were an essential factor in determining the course of the Zionist struggle.

# ❧ Yolande

Most of the houses on suliman avenue in the center of Cairo's European district were usually dark by 3 A.M., but an attractive, young divorcee known as Yolande Gabay would often entertain journalists, diplomats, and army officers at her home until well past that hour. Her weekly receptions were on the must list of every newly arrived diplomat or correspondent interested in cultivating important connections. Egyptian statesmen were also in regular attendance at Yolande's salon and welcomed the chance to sound out the foreigners on the British occupation and other issues.

The conversation ranged from gossip about Cairo personalities and King Farouk's dancing girls to the Allied war effort, Egyptian politics, and court intrigues. It was 1943 and thousands of foreign soldiers were stationed in the Egyptian capital, the strategic nerve center of the Second World War where the allied command plotted its Mediterranean operations.

Yolande's family were of Spanish-Italian origin, and, like most wealthy Jews in Cairo at that time, lived in a large house surrounded by walls and attended by many servants. Although her father was Orthodox, Yolande felt little identification with Judaism and was largely ignorant of her people's history and customs. She had finished secondary school in Cairo and was enrolled at the Sorbonne when her parents called her home from Paris. They had arranged a marriage with a wealthy businessman whom Yolande had never met. This practice was not unusual among Egypt's Jews, but Yolande could accept neither her husband nor the restricted, bourgeois life of Cairo's gallicized Jews. She was of a romantic nature and yearned for excitement. Her husband tried earnestly to make her happy but the match had been doomed from the outset. Even the birth of a son, Gilbert, did little to cement their relationship. Finally they divorced and Yolande moved into a comfortable house with Gilbert and set about trying to forget her unhappy marriage. She was fond of dining out, dancing, and swimming and often passed her days with friends who shared these interests.

There were at first few men who interested Yolande, but then she began meeting Palestinian Jews and realized that, unlike the Levantine Jewish men she had always known, the Palestinian males were straightforward, virile types who seemed to possess a firmness and dedication that greatly attracted her. Most of these Palestinians had been trained by the Jewish underground defense organization known as the Haganah, and when the war broke out they had volunteered for service with the British army. Many of them were being posted to assignments in Cairo and found in Yolande's home a place where they could relax and enjoy the company of a warm and sympathetic woman. As Yolande spent more and more time with these men, she found that a new spirit seemed to animate her; somehow she felt that their presence suggested a new meaning to her life. Their conversation excited her as they spoke of the need to open a second front in the West against Hitler and of rescue operations involving the smuggling of Jews across borders and parachuting behind

Nazi lines to organize armed Jewish resistance. In time these men were to change Yolande's life completely.

Her first opportunity to serve Israel's cause was provided by Enzo Sereni, an Italian-born Palestinian who had first come to the attention of the Haganah because of his Italian background and leadership qualities. In 1943, when the Haganah began dropping paratroopers behind German lines in an effort to rouse Jewish resistance, Sereni was selected to be among the first Palestinians to enter Italy. He was sent to Cairo and trained as a paratrooper by British army instructors. The command of the British Psychological Warfare Division expressed an interest in Enzo's Italian assignment and proposed that he broadcast propaganda programs designed to encourage the anti-Fascist forces and civilian population of Italy. Everything was going well in preparing Sereni for his mission and the cooperation of the Italian underground had been secured when Enzo suddenly disappeared without a trace.

The British authorities searched for him in vain, and it was widely speculated that he had either been killed or kidnapped by Egyptian Fascists. Yolande's help was enlisted by the Haganah, and thanks to her connections with government officials she was able to arrange for a search of Cairo's prisons. Enzo was found in one of them under a different name. He had been kidnapped and imprisoned on false charges by Fascist agents who hoped to prevent his proposed broadcasts on behalf of the Allies.

The Palestinian was cleared and freed after the British military authorities intervened. He completed his training and left for Italy where he was captured soon after landing. Enzo's death at the hands of the Italian Fascists had a profound effect on Yolande, who had been captivated by his courage and charm. His strong feeling for Palestine had awakened in her a desire to visit the Promised Land,

and shortly after his death she left Cairo for a vacation in Palestine.

To the leaders of the Haganah who followed her movements, Yolande seemed to be just another tourist staying at luxury hotels, dining in good restaurants, sight-seeing, and passing her evenings in nightclubs. To the necessarily stern and abstemious officers of the Jewish defense organization, Yolande was a good-looking, frivolous woman, and it surprised these dedicated underground fighters that their revered late comrade Enzo had told them Yolande was trustworthy.

In the beginning of 1944, Yaacov Tsur of the Jewish Agency* was given the task of opening an office in Cairo for the purpose of representing Zionist interests in the Egyptian capital. Ostensibly the office was to serve as a service club for Palestinian Jewish soldiers stationed in Egypt.

Tsur was told to seek Yolande's assistance in all dealings with Egyptian authorities, but he, too, was disappointed by her vivacious and playful manner. Like the leaders of the Haganah, Tsur was the product of rough-hewn, idealistic, puritanical society and he was impatient with the superficial customs of what he considered decadent European culture.

But Enzo Sereni had been a more perceptive judge of people than his comrades. He had been capable of realizing how certain circumstances could stir people like Yolande. He had appreciated the qualities of devotion and faith possessed by many young Egyptian Jews, who, discontented with the vapid existence surrounding them, sought a meaningful relationship to their Judaism.

At the same time as Tsur assumed his assignment, a Haganah officer named Levi Avrahami arrived in the

* The Jewish administrative body in mandate Palestine. Following independence in 1948, the Agency evolved into a quasi-governmental body dealing with immigration, absorption, and Zionist educational activities throughout the world.

Egyptian capital. His family had been in Palestine for
several generations and he knew the country well. More-
over, he was familiar with Arab customs and spoke Arabic
fluently.

Avrahami belonged to the generation of Haganah fighters
who had witnessed the days of Arab nationalist agitation
during the late 1930's, when unarmed Jewish settlements
were frequently attacked by Arabs from neighboring villages.
Tens of thousands of Jews who had fled Hitler arrived in
Palestine during that time, and Arab leaders incited their
followers to oppose Jewish immigration. The motive
behind this was the desire of the Fascist Italians and
Germans to challenge Britain's mandate in Palestine and
her position in the Middle East. To further this end, agents
in the employ of the Italian and German propaganda
ministries bribed key Arab leaders to promote dissension
within Palestine. England, however, wished to delimit the
Middle Eastern front and avoid any responsibility for protecting the Jewish community. The British Foreign Office,
acting on the recommendations of the mandate authorities,
made it clear that insofar as His Majesty's government
was concerned, the policy of encouraging the establishment
of a Jewish national home in Palestine in accordance with
the Balfour Declaration was now a dead issue. British
apathy only served to encourage violent Arab attacks on
Jewish settlements. The Jews fortified and defended their
holdings as best they could but did not dare take the offensive.

Gradually, however, a change took place in the thinking
of the Haganah, for the leaders of the Jewish settlement
had perceived that the Arabs would leave them alone only
if their provocations were answered with force. Ord
Wingate, the celebrated British commander, had become
a champion of the Jews and was a strong advocate of
Jewish self-defense organizations. He organized Haganah

night squads, and these clandestine bands of dedicated Jewish youth served to frighten the hostile Arabs and persuade them that the Jews could go on the offensive.

Levi Avrahami arrived in Cairo disguised as a British army captain. Despite his loneliness in this alien city full of enemy agents, spies, informers, and Egyptian intelligence operatives, he avoided the many friends he had among the Palestinian officers stationed there, as he was afraid that their affectionate curiosity would compromise his cover.

Several months after his arrival he communicated with Yolande and arranged to meet at her home. At first he was guarded as they began to discuss his mission, but soon they fell into easy conversation so that they hardly noticed the time passing.

Nightfall came and still they talked. Yolande made cup after cup of the sweet, thick Turkish coffee that always accompanies conversation in the Orient. Until well past midnight they sat and talked and while doing so discovered each other. Levi was anxious to understand Yolande's motives for wanting to work for the Haganah. He asked her many personal questions, as he was determined to convince himself that this pretty woman was sincere in her devotion to the Jewish cause and not just an adventuress seeking a thrill to relieve the ennui and disappointment of her life. He had to have complete trust in her, and after several hours, listening to Yolande talk of her life and her ideas for helping Israel, Levi was sure she would never betray him.

The next morning they left by car for Alexandria to look for a villa that could be suitably disguised to serve as a depot for the arms and matériel to be gathered by Haganah agents from the heaps of armaments littering the battlegrounds of the western Egyptian desert. The villa would be a central collection point from which small transport convoys would leave for Tel Aviv as frequently as security considerations allowed.

After a three-day search they found what seemed to be the ideal house—a secluded, two-story villa surrounded by a wall of trees. Yolande immediately set to fixing it up. They decided to disguise it as a health resort for Allied soldiers. Avrahami was impressed by Yolande's calm efficiency, and as their collaboration progressed, he couldn't help but wonder at the quiet ease with which she undertook even the most difficult assignments. She had a gracious and winning way with people, and even strangers quickly warmed to her and sought to please her. Her circle of friends was extraordinarily wide and embraced family, social acquaintances, Egyptian journalists, foreign correspondents, Egyptian statesmen, Arab ambassadors and their aides, and high-ranking British and Egyptian army officers. She was always in demand for cocktail parties and dinners.

At Avrahami's suggestion, Yolande began submitting articles on the political situation in Egypt to several French publications. Her work gained acceptance, and she was able to receive accreditation as a correspondent.

One of her first important interviews was with Azam Pasha, secretary of the Arab League. The idea for her to meet this important Arab dignitary had come from Mohi Bey, one of Azam's assistants and a friend of Yolande whom she had met while they were students at the Sorbonne. When Mohi met Yolande again in Cairo and learned that she had become a correspondent, he suggested that she meet his boss. Azam reacted favorably to the suggestion since he was anxious to organize the League along accepted political lines. He appreciated the importance of publicity in the foreign press.

As an Egyptian, Azam viewed the League as a means of increasing his country's influence in the world. His approach, however, was not a narrow, nationalistic one; he regarded Egypt's power as an integral part of the potential strength of the entire Arab world. In his talk with Yolande he expressed the hope that the League would bring about negotiations for the withdrawal of British forces. In heavily accented French he expressed himself as a forceful and candid advocate of the Arab position. In little more than an hour Azam Pasha covered the whole panorama of Anglo-Egyptian relations.

Yolande learned a great deal from the interview, and characteristically the Arab League secretary mentioned many things off the record in order to ingratiate himself with a foreign correspondent.

Azam had talked about the great wave of anticolonial feeling that would engulf the world after the war. Yolande realized that he was right in predicting the agitation against British rule in several Arab countries. Egypt would surely be a focal point in the Arab quest for independence from the British.

In Palestine the Haganah, which represented the labor Zionist movement, and the Irgun, the military arm of the right-wing Zionist Revisionists, observed a truce with the English for the duration of the war. But the LEHI—the Freedom Fighters of Israel—refused to suspend the struggle. This small clandestine group of fanatic terrorists had been organized by Abraham Stern, a classics scholar and linguist who abandoned his studies in the early 1930's to participate in Jewish underground activities. A subsequent dispute over tactics and revolutionary doctrine led him to break with the Revisionist Zionist leader Zeev Jabotinsky and form his own band of rebels, which in time came to be known by the British and in the West as "the Stern Gang."

Even after Stern's death at the hands of the British in 1942, the group continued its liberation struggle. Sternists performed daring sabotage operations in strategic locations, assassinated British personnel, and in 1944 carried out an astounding act that was to focus the world's attention on the Zionist struggle and was even to arouse pro-Jewish sentiment among the Arabs: the assassination of Lord Moyne, the British minister of state in the Middle East, at his home in Cairo.

The assassins were two young Palestinians, Eliahu Bet Zouri and Eliahu Hakim. At their trial they used the prisoners' dock as a platform from which they eloquently and virulently condemned British policy in the Middle East. Accusing His Majesty's government of abandoning thousands of Jews to their deaths, they specifically charged Anthony Eden, British foreign secretary, with responsibility for this policy and blamed Lord Moyne, who, as representative of the British cabinet in the Middle East, was responsible for its implementation.

By virtue of the stoic and dignified behavior of the defendants at the trial, the considerable coverage the Egyptian press and radio devoted to the proceedings, the motives of the accused, and the revelations of British intrigue in the area, Egyptian public opinion was aroused to the point of openly expressing sympathy with the anti-British struggle of the Zionists. For months the trial was a major topic of conversations in the cafés of Cairo and Alexandria and engaged the full-time attention of the Egyptian cabinet.

The Egyptians had found an outlet for their resentment of Britain's continued occupation and colonial attitude. British demands that the Egyptian authorities hand over the two assassins were refused with the reply that the accused had committed a crime on Egyptian soil and would therefore be tried by an Egyptian court. The fate of the two Jewish terrorists had become a rallying point for Egypt's own independence movement.

In response to this increasing nationalist sentiment,

the British had begun to exert behind-the-scenes pressure on Ahmed Maher Pasha, the Egyptian premier, and insisted that the accused be given the death sentence. Until the last stages of the trial Maher withstood outside pressures and saw to it that the proceedings were conducted fairly, but in the end Britain's determination to obtain the maximum punishment for the Sternists prevailed. Bet Zouri and Hakim were finally hanged after Maher Pasha had granted three stays of execution and had even assured the Egyptian Jewish community that he would do everything in his power to pardon the two young men.

For Yolande the Moyne assassination and the executions were a shocking experience. She had never admired the Stern Gang, but the fate of the two Eliahus brought home to her the tragedy of the Jewish people. She felt outrage and impotence in the face of the Nazi holocaust and the murder of millions of Jews. She vowed that she would do anything she could for her people.

For the next two years she assisted Avrahami in arranging the illegal entry into Palestine of thousands of Jews—Egyptian, North African, and European—in defiance of the British ban on Jewish immigration. She helped the Haganah officer recruit people who could buy automobiles and trucks and register them under false names, people who knew whom to bribe and for how much, people who could forge official documents and transport groups of refugees without being caught by the British police.

By mid 1946 the Palestine question once again became a crucial issue, following Britain's indication that she intended to leave Palestine. The sincerity of the British was doubted, and Whitehall's diplomatic maneuvering in Washington, at the United Nations, in Arab capitals, and in Palestine left many questions unanswered. As the future government of Israel, the Jewish Agency was faced with new challenges at the end of the war. The Anglo-American

Commission on Palestine had completed its fact-finding tour of the Middle East and was about to present its recommendations which were to serve as the basis for settling the Palestine issue. In order to plan for any contingency, it was vital for the Jewish Agency to know in advance of the commission's consensus, and it was equally important for the Jewish leaders to know what action the Arabs would take vis-à-vis the commission. Haganah intelligence services had to obtain information from the Arab capitals, particularly Cairo. The major question confronting the Jewish Agency was whether or not it would be possible to capitalize on the pro-Zionist sentiment and goodwill expressed among certain Egyptian circles, especially at the time of the Moyne assassination trial, as a significant element in achieving a peaceful solution for the Palestine question.

Levi Avrahami was required to furnish the Agency with weekly résumés of political discussions in Cairo and elsewhere in the Arab world. This was a time of increased diplomatic activity, because in addition to the Palestine issue, Anglo-Egyptian discussions concerning Britain's withdrawal from Egyptian bases were renewed.

The British continued to manipulate Egyptian political figures in an attempt to bring about the appointment of pro-British ministers who would prove amenable to compromise. At the same time the Arab League carried on intensive political activity as part of its goal to free the Middle East of British and French domination. Cairo was the scene of frequent meetings involving Arab kings, princes, and high-ranking emissaries, as the League developed the organization of its various sections and worked out a coordinated plan of action.

In Jerusalem leaders of the Jewish Agency, such as David Ben-Gurion, Moshe Sharett, and Eliezer Kaplan, sought contacts with Arab leaders. In Palestine their attempts were thwarted by the extremists led by the Mufti of Jerusalem, Haj Amin El Husseini. The more moderate Palestinian Arabs, including the Nashashibi family, trade unionists, and Arab members of the Jewish Histadrut Labor Federation, were terrorized by the Mufti's gangs and several were found murdered. The Jewish leadership sought to establish direct contact with the leaders of Egypt and other Arab states in an attempt to find some ground for a rapprochement with the Palestinian Arabs. The fruitful exchange of letters between King Feisal of Iraq and Chaim Weizmann twenty years earlier and the evidence of Egyptian sympathy for the Moyne assassins, as well as the fact that the Egyptian press was almost completely free of anti-Jewish or anti-Zionist sentiment, gave them cause to hope that a direct approach to Egyptian leadership might prove successful.

Yolande received instructions to supplement Levi's reports with summaries of political developments in Cairo. Eventually she was supplying Jerusalem with reports based on direct interviews with key figures. Gradually she employed a few assistants who also supplied firsthand accounts based on contacts with Egyptian politicians, foreign diplomats, and newspaper editors. Yolande had succeeded in developing a network of informants and contacts and had also developed her friendship with Mohi Bey, taking advantage of the Arab League official's fondness for her. Bey was equally at home in Arabic and French and bore the intense expression of a fervent Arab nationalist and intellectual. He regarded his relations with Yolande as symbolic of the medieval golden age of Islam when Jews and Moslems lived together in harmony.

In the meantime Yolande had arranged to cover the Egyptian capital for the English-language *Palestine Post* published in Jerusalem. This additional journalistic credential enabled her to move about freely and arrange interviews with whomever she wanted. As a correspondent for the *Palestine Post,* she had an ample excuse for asking detailed questions pertaining to Palestine and the Arab League.

The queries poured in from Haganah intelligence in Jerusalem, and Yolande, with the help of her network of informants, kept the Jewish Agency chiefs supplied with a steady stream of important information.

From Mohi Bey she learned that Azam Pasha, the secretary of the Arab League whom she had previously interviewed, was holding discussions with Arab heads of state at an emergency meeting at the Lebanese summer resort of Inshias. There at the pine-covered mountain retreat the League members were working out a program of joint action to be implemented in the event that the Anglo-American commission recommended the establishment of a Jewish state in Palestine. At Arab League headquarters in Cairo, military and economic experts prepared reports on the various aspects of this one question. The pace was feverish and all-night sessions were common.

Yolande tried to keep up with the progress of the League's researchers and report every development to Palestine. Patiently she would piece together scraps of information obtained from friends of Mohi in the League secretariat. Although she was able to provide Avrahami with a general picture of how the Arabs planned to exert pressure on the commission, she was less than satisfied with the quality of the reports being transmitted to Jerusalem. She decided that she would attempt to get her hands on the original Arab League documents rather than rely on secondhand sources of information. She was determined that the Jewish community of Palestine would not be caught unawares.

The summer of 1946 was the hottest Egypt had experienced in forty years. One morning in late August, Yolande called Avrahami at his apartment and invited him to her summer cottage. With her in the car when she picked him up were her son, Gilbert, and Mohi Bey. Avrahami greeted the Arab League official, and they engaged in small talk as Yolande speeded through the desert. By noon they had arrived at a group of cottages on the shores of the Nile and were greeted at one of the houses by an elderly Egyptian servant. Mohi excused himself and retired to one of the rooms where he spent the afternoon going over his files while Yolande, Gilbert, and Avrahami went swimming and sailing. At supper the conversation was devoted mainly to the problems of the Middle East. Mohi said that the Arab states would soon win their independence whether England wanted them to or not. He spoke as an Arab patriot who, while aware of his people's shortcomings and the weakness of their leaders, was also proud of the Arabs' great scientific and cultural achievements. Avrahami noted Mohi's obvious intimacy with Yolande.

Just before going to bed, Yolande pressed Avrahami's hand and whispered, "*Au revoir.*" More puzzled than ever, he went to sleep and awoke shortly before dawn to the sound of a car. Looking out through the shades, he saw Yolande, Mohi, and Gilbert driving off. Angry and confused, he ran out of his room and found an envelope on a table near the living room. It was a note from Yolande: "Just in case you're upset, I've left you a little consolation present in the closet."

In the closet was Mohi's briefcase, containing documents arranged by subject matter and bearing the labels "classified," "secret," "top secret."

Avrahami was incredulous. He quickly thumbed through the files, memorizing the subject headings. For years he, Yolande, and the other Jewish agents in Egypt had worked hard to obtain information and details on the inner workings of the Arab League. The work had been laborious,

painstaking, and, at best, piecemeal. Now in front of him
was the complete setup. Here were the most up-to-date
documents: correspondence between Arab kings and their
nonroyal counterparts, the Arab League's position on the
Palestine question, plans for circumventing the recommendations of the Anglo-American Commission should it
decide in favor of a Jewish state, estimates of the Haganah's military preparedness.

Avrahami decided not to lose any time. He gathered up
the papers, closed the briefcase, and left a note for Yolande: "Thanks for the present. I had to return to Cairo
and I couldn't leave it behind. I'll call you." He locked the
cottage and took a taxi back to the capital. By the time he
reached the city, he had decided to find a photographer
whom he could trust to make photocopies of all the papers.
When he was finished and had arranged to have the copies
delivered to Jerusalem, he telephoned Yolande several
times until he reached her late that night. By this time he
was desperately worried about returning the briefcase. He
was astonished. She sounded cheerful and relaxed. She
asked him how he had spent the day, and when he tried to
hint about returning the briefcase, she changed the subject.
At first he thought that someone was in the room; maybe
Mohi was at her side. But Yolande continued to chatter
away, and Levi Avrahami realized that all had been arranged with Mohi beforehand. Out of his love for Yolande
and his dedication to a peaceful solution of Arab-Jewish
differences, Mohi Bey had risked his career.

In Jerusalem the Jewish Agency's Arab experts studied
the photocopies of the League's documents day and night.
Never had they obtained such valuable intelligence. A
whole new perspective emerged from a study of the papers.
Several attitudes were challenged, and certain Arab personalities were seen in a new light. Most significant was the
indication of a surprisingly restrained attitude among

certain key Arab figures as far as the Palestine question was concerned. A lack of enmity towards the Jewish people was revealed. This was especially true of some Egyptian leaders. As a result of these new findings, the Jewish Agency directors decided to take advantage of the favorable predisposition of several of the League members and send an envoy to Cairo to begin talks on the Palestine issue. Eliahu Sassoon, the Jewish Agency's Arab affairs expert, was selected for the mission.

Yolande was directed to facilitate Sassoon's assignment by arranging meetings with Egyptian officials. The Agency sought to soften or neutralize Egypt's stand concerning proposals for partitioning Palestine and establishing a Jewish state. The highest priority was given to a meeting with Ali Maher, Egypt's premier and a central figure in Egyptian politics for many years.

Yolande was granted an interview with Maher, and while ostensibly conducting the routine newspaper-like question-and-answer confrontation, she skillfully brought the conversation around to the Palestine question and Egypt's feelings on the matter. Maher was in a mellow mood and he began reminiscing. He recalled his meeting with Dr. Weizmann and the strong impression the Zionist leader had made on him. He spoke of Ben-Gurion and said with an element of pride: "Do you really think the British called the St. James conference on Palestine? I suggested it." He was referring to Britain's attempt in 1939, on the eve of the Second World War, to bring together Arab and Jewish representatives in London in an effort to achieve a détente on the Palestine issue. It was the first time that Egypt had taken part in these discussions.

Yolande complimented him on his political acumen and asked in an innocent tone: "Your Excellency, one of the foremost experts on Arab affairs in the Jewish Agency, Eliahu Sassoon, is due to arrive in Cairo soon. You've probably heard of him. He's the same Syrian Jew who was such an eloquent spokesman for the Arab nationalist movement in Damascus. I'm one of his many admirers in the Middle East and he's a good friend of mine. I'm sure that both of you would be interested in talking. Such a meeting could pave the way to peace between Jew and Arab."

This was a difficult time for Ali Maher. Anglo-Egyptian talks on the withdrawal of the British from Suez were a continual on-again-off-again deal. Sidki Pasha, a former Egyptian premier, had fomented a government crisis by agitating for British withdrawal by a specific date. The British hoped that Maher would follow a moderate line and agree on a compromise allowing the British to maintain a form of presence in Suez. The Egyptian press and radio were full of angry denunciations of the British, and street demonstrations by students of El Azhar University were becoming a daily occurrence. Maher was caught in between. A meeting with a representative of the Jewish Agency was a highly unlikely prospect in view of the tense atmosphere in the Egyptian capital.

Yolande, however, prevailed. She relentlessly stressed the common aspiration of Jews and Arabs to be rid of their colonial master. This shared goal engaged Egyptian interest with the result that, when Sassoon arrived in Cairo, he had before him a heavy schedule of meetings with Egyptian leaders and important representatives of other Arab governments. The confrontation with Maher was the high point of the Zionist emissary's visit. Despite the rather strained circumstances of the meeting, the tone of discussion was moderate, Sassoon, a prominent Sephardic Jew and outstanding Arabist, felt a sense of historic mission.

Maher listened attentively and reflected on the significance of this meeting—the premier of Egypt, the leading nation of the Arab world, was talking to a representative of the Jewish Agency in the heart of Cairo and discussing the establishment of a Jewish state. He could hardly believe it.

Sassoon's argument was simple: A Jewish state wouldn't endanger or conflict with any Egyptian interest. On the contrary, the founding of Israel would aid Egypt's struggle for independence, for Israel would be able to influence foreign public opinion in favor of Egypt and would also promise future cooperation and generous assistance.

The meeting was coming to an end, and Sassoon believed that he had effected a valuable contact, one worth preserving. He rose and, in the ornate style peculiar to the Arabic language, addressed the Egyptian premier: "Sir, it is possible that it is your destiny to serve as a historic intermediary, a harbinger of a new epoch for our two peoples; I would deem it a great honor if you would allow me to invite Messrs. Ben-Gurion and Sharett to meet with you to exchange views on our common problems. May I be permitted to take the initiative in this matter?"

Ali Maher thought for a minute and replied: "I'd like to discuss the questions you've raised with Azam Pasha, the secretary of the Arab League, and I'd also like to talk to King Saud. Afterward I'll get in touch with you. It will be better that way."

The meeting ended on that note. It was clear that the Egyptian leader did not wish to be solely responsible for further talks with Jewish leaders. Nevertheless, Sassoon felt that Maher's attitude had been favorable and sufficiently encouraging.

"It can be said that Egypt under Ali Maher would not view the establishment of Israel as a hostile act and certainly not as a provocative act leading to a violent response like war," read Sassoon's optimistic report to Ben-Gurion, Sharett, and Kaplan.

His subsequent talks seemed to justify this conclusion. Amid the frenetic political activity going on in Cairo at that time, Yolande had accomplished the impossible. Sassoon and his associates were overwhelmed with her success in arranging meeting after meeting with Arab leaders.

Sassoon returned to Jerusalem with a rather encouraging assessment. As far as he could ascertain, the Palestine question was not of paramount importance to Egypt's leaders. Nor was Egyptian public opinion preoccupied with it. He had found the Arab leaders he had conferred with to be restrained and moderate. The fact that they had agreed to grant an interview to a representative of the Jewish Agency supported Sassoon's optimism.

Following Sassoon's diplomatic opening, Eliahu Eilat and other prominent Zionist envoys arrived in Cairo to observe Egyptian political developments at first hand and to encourage the moderate elements whenever possible.

Unfortunately a shift in Arab feeling took place shortly thereafter. Ali Maher was dismissed from office, and the more extremist factions called for action against the Zionists. Compared to those who came later, these extremists could still be called relatively restrained, for they contented themselves with calling for volunteers to assist the Arabs of Palestine and raising funds to retain land that was being purchased by the Jewish Agency. Despite their efforts, Egyptian public opinion was not particularly aroused on the Palestine issue. In Jerusalem it was hoped that the extremist element would remain an ineffectual, if highly vocal, minority.

Although Yolande lacked political sophistication, she could sense an impending change. Her Egyptian friends still received her cordially, and she still arranged meetings with representatives of the Jewish Agency. Her position as correspondent for the *Palestine Post* was not challenged, and her secret activities in the Haganah's intelligence apparatus continued to produce successful results.

It was no longer a small undertaking. Her contacts had by this time been developed to a point at which anything pertaining to Palestine, whether it originated with the Arab League or an Egyptian ministry, quickly became known to Yolande. The machine ran smoothly. Week after week the Jewish Agency's Arab experts were supplied with abundant material.

In 1947, Jerusalem eagerly awaited the Anglo-American Commission's recommendations for settling the Palestine dispute. For the Jews the commission represented the hope for a Jewish state. The Arabs for the most part boycotted the commission's hearings, and the Jewish Agency could see that further political activity was necessary in order to soften the stand of Arab leaders—at least those of Egypt—insofar as the commission was concerned. At the same time, however, Ben-Gurion and other Agency officials were worried about Yolande's safety. They were convinced that she took too many risks and would soon be arrested. She was ordered to prepare herself for a sudden departure from Egypt.

Yolande interpreted their concern as proof of how important it was for her to remain at her post. Daily she received conflicting reports from her informers. From summaries of Egyptian intelligence reports it seemed that they had no real idea of Zionist activity in their midst. The oriental imagination was very much in evidence in the various exaggerated estimates of the military strength of Haganah units in Palestine. The Egyptian intelligence agencies also seemed to be unable to pinpoint correctly the location of many Jewish border settlements. These incompetent Egyptian assessments gave Jewish leaders the impression that Egypt was not prepared for war.

Yolande was in a disconsolate mood following her tragic love affair with Albert Hermor, a South African officer she had met early in 1947 on the beach at Alexandria. They had spent the day sailing and by sunset were both in love. He was a major stationed in Libya and was in Egypt for a short vacation. The next few days were the happiest in Yolande's life as she gave herself completely to this stranger. She knew little of his background and asked few questions. He did likewise, and Yolande's frequent phone calls to Cairo provoked no inquiries. She was grateful for his discretion and trusted him completely. Even her son Gilbert sensed the difference and knew that for the first time his mother was happy.

When it came to say goodbye, Yolande accompanied her lover to the airport. The Major proposed to her and she accepted.

The next morning Yolande was called to the hospital in Cairo. Albert Hermor's plane had crashed and he was in serious condition. All night he repeated Yolande's name in a state of delirium. Somehow the hospital staff had been able to trace her by searching throughout Cairo.

For over a month she spent several hours each day by his bedside, feeding him and changing his bandages. The doctors had given him up, but after a few weeks he began to show signs of recovery. He finally left the hospital with Yolande, and when he had regained some of his strength, they flew to Ramat David in Palestine's Jezreel Valley where a friend of Hermor's was serving. They stayed on a nearby farm, and when the South African was strong enough, they rented a car and toured the country. When they were in Jerusalem, Yolande told him about her activities in Egypt and the reason for the many calls to Cairo. She wanted him to understand everything, and he responded with great interest and a willingness to help the Jewish cause. Yolande's happiness could not have been greater.

After their vacation in Palestine they spent a week in Alexandria before leaving for Tripoli where Yolande was to wait for Hermor while he arranged his discharge from the army elsewhere in Libya.

Hermor never returned. The last she heard from him

was a short telegram he had sent just before departing for
Tripoli:

> My darling. By the time you receive this telegram, I'll
> be holding you in my arms and we'll read it together. I
> just had to send you a telegram when I left. I thank God
> that I have you. I need you.
>
> Love,
> Albert

She was brought to a British army hospital. His plane
had crashed. Once again Yolande hoped for a miracle, but
Hermor never regained consciousness and died a few hours
later.

Avrahami understood Yolande's sadness over her imminent departure from Egypt. She would have to leave her
home and the place where Hermor was buried, as well as
her friends and family.

They reviewed their operation and resolved to intensify
their efforts to obtain information on the Arab League's
Palestine policy, for they knew that a turning point was
near. Measures were taken to evacuate key personnel who
had already fallen under suspicion. They decided to improve their contacts with the court, as it was apparent that
King Farouk was gaining a greater say in affairs of state.

The Mufti of Jerusalem was in Cairo talking to Hassan
Al Banah, head of Ikhwan, the fanatic, right-wing, Moslem
brotherhood, and to leaders of Misr El Fatat, the Fascist
youth organization that had been openly pro-Nazi during
the war.

Jewish agents in Cairo soon discovered that, as a result
of his talks with extremist Arab leaders, the Mufti had
obtained volunteers and arms for the Palestinian Arabs.
The Jewish Agency immediately brought pressure to bear
on the United States State Department, and as a result the
Mufti, who had been living in Farouk's villa at Hiluan as
a house guest, was forced to restrict his activities and

temper his anti-Jewish tirades. In those days a diplomatic note from the United States carried weight in Cairo, especially since the Egyptians wanted American assistance in arranging for a speedy British troop withdrawal.

The reports forwarded by Avrahami and Yolande to Jerusalem still indicated that Egypt preferred not to be drawn into a war in Palestine in spite of the Mufti and Arab extremists.

Unfortunately the influence of the moderates was on the wane, and Yolande and her confederates, realizing this, decided openly to cultivate those figures who were the last hope for preventing Egyptian intervention in Palestine. Yolande spoke to practically every accessible political personality in Cairo. Their courtesy and ostensible sympathy occasionally made her feel optimistic over the future of a Jewish state. Meanwhile Jerusalem was kept busy with a continual flow of reports and appraisals based on these Cairo meetings. Yolande still felt there was a chance Egypt would remain neutral. While no important leader spoke in favor of the establishment of a Jewish state in Palestine, there was as yet no real hostility or warlike intention displayed by Egyptian leaders.

Once again she saw Azam Pasha, secretary of the Arab League. She had no mandate from the Jewish Agency for these talks and often conducted them without any instructions from Jerusalem. During her talk with Azam Pasha, she was asked to inform the Jewish Agency that the Arab League was supporting Libyan independence and an expression of like support from the Agency would be considered an example of the Jewish community's positive intentions toward the Arab world. Libya's future was the cause of a major diplomatic battle being waged by Rome and London and other powers over the former Italian colony.

Yolande's answer, "Our strength and influence are limited,

but we will be ready to display our good will," satisfied Azam
for the time being.

Even though the Agency kept Yolande's promise in the
Libyan matter, later talks with Azam proved disappointing.
He finally told Yolande that there didn't seem to be any solution to the Palestine problem and the only course of action
was for the Arab League to accept responsibility for the
contested area until such time as the Jews and Palestinian
Arabs could reach a settlement. IIis statement came as a
shock to Yolande. Anything would be preferable to having
the Arab League govern the Jews of Palestine.

The special emissaries of the Jewish Agency, chief among
them Eliahu Sassoon, soon lost their optimism. The hopes
their missions had raised were disappointed. They had dared
to hope that the Arab countries would not resort to war to
prevent the establishment of Israel.

Pressure for armed opposition to the Zionists mounted in
Cairo following the Anglo-American Commission of Inquiry's recommendation for the founding of a bi-national
Arab-Jewish state in Palestine. The irregular Arab forces
in Palestine, who had already experienced the armed determination of the Haganah, clamored for arms and volunteers.
Extremist groups in Cairo pressured the Egyptian officer
corps, the air force in particular. They insisted that Jewish
border settlements and transportation centers be bombed.
Large quantities of Egyptian arms were being forwarded to
the Palestinian Arabs while British mandate forces closed
their eyes to these illegal shipments.

Yolande learned that King Farouk would attend the Arab
League meeting at the Lebanese mountain resort of Inshias
in the summer of 1947. It was clear that with Farouk
present, the conference would turn into a Pan-Arab summit
with one subject on the agenda: how to prevent the establishment of a Jewish state in Palestine.

The summit took place in great secrecy, but when the

Arab kings and premiers returned to their respective capitals, the newspapers were calling for war against the Jews, a sure indication that the Inshias meeting had decided to back the Palestinian Arabs with men and arms.

Jewish Agency leaders were still reluctant to believe that the Arabs would go to war. They attached greater importance to the conflict between President Harry Truman and Foreign Minister Ernest Bevin over the Anglo-American Commission recommendations than to what they regarded as empty Arab threats. American public opinion was strongly in favor of a Jewish state.

The day after Farouk's return to Cairo from Inshias, Yolande managed to send Jerusalem a fairly accurate account of the Arab summit based on talks with her contacts at court. According to her dispatch, not all of the Arabs meeting in Lebanon were in accord with the proposal of the extremists that a united Arab force be deployed against the Jews. Although they had misgivings over the prospect of war, some Arab leaders, notably King Abdullah of Jordan, were influenced by the promise of gaining additional territory.

The president of Lebanon, Bishara El Hori, suggested that the Arabs lay their case before the United Nations. He was convinced that nations friendly to the Arab cause would reject any proposal entailing the establishment of a Jewish state. He was the only leader at Inshias who openly advocated political action rather than force of arms.

The other Arabs dismissed Hori as a typical Lebanese statesman, trying to protect the delicate balance in his country between Christians and Moslems. They knew that tiny Lebanon was anxious to avoid any risks.

"Who is the enemy? The Jews or the English?" Shuki El Kuatley, the president of Syria, challenged the summit meeting. "In another two days the Grand Mufti of Jerusalem will be here. He will speak in the name of the noble Arab warriors whose blood has been shed for Jerusalem. He will ask us what we intend to do and how we propose to oppose the Anglo-American proposals calling for the establishment of a Jewish state. 'We have no choice,' the Mufti will say. 'We can only fight with arms.' We have to decide now: are we ready to fight and, if so, against whom—the Jews or the English or both?"

The leaders were suspicious of one another. Farouk wanted to hear how the others felt before committing himself. Abdullah of Jordan hoped through British passivity to increase his territory by annexing Jerusalem and the West Bank. He openly stated that Jordan was opposed to force but at the same time gave secret orders to his army, the Arab Legion, to remain in a state of alert.

Emir Saud, the son of King Saud of Saudi Arabia, said that he was not empowered to speak for his father, but he indicated that the desert king was prepared to send armed units to war.

Farouk, after much hesitation, conceded that he could not tell the Arabs of Palestine not to revolt but added that revolt would be an illegal action.

Yolande's report to Jerusalem described the confusion of the conference. The representatives of Iraq and Saudi Arabia were the most extreme, while Egypt, Jordan, and Lebanon—nations bordering on Palestine—seemed anxious to avoid military confrontation. The meeting ended with a decision to call another Arab summit. One piece of business enacted was a recommendation of economic and diplomatic sanctions against England and the United States to coerce them into opposing the partition plan. It was also decided to send arms and volunteers to the Palestinian Arabs.

Events moved swiftly after the conference. Without warning, the extremists in Egypt took matters into their own hands. Hassan Al Banah, the head of the right-wing Moslem brotherhood, ordered the first Egyptian volunteers to Pales-

tine. Al Banah's action was followed by a declaration of
*jihad*—a holy war—by Misr El Fatat, the Fascist youth
organization.

Yolande was bitterly disappointed. She saw that her efforts to reach a reconciliation with the Arabs had failed.

Meanwhile, Abdullah, in close cooperation with the British, decided to annex Jerusalem and that part of Palestine
that had been designated for an Arab state as soon as the
British relinquished their mandate.

King Farouk, who also had plans for territorial expansion,
was aware of Abdullah's intentions. He allowed himself to
be carried along by the national frenzy precipitated by the
extremists. Arab mobs demonstrated in the streets, and a
steady flow of matériel and soldiers to Palestine gave proof
of Egypt's warlike stance. The first press reports of large-
scale armed encounters between Jews and Arabs in Palestine added to Egypt's general hysteria.

The decision of the General Assembly in November, 1947,
to partition Palestine into Jewish and Arab states prompted
Azam Pasha to call a secret emergency meeting of the Arab
League. Azam cited the recommendations of the Inshias
conference and told the delegates that if Britain and the
United States went along with the General Assembly resolution, it would be necessary for every League member to
break off economic, cultural, and diplomatic ties with these
two powers. Despite the reservations expressed by several
representatives, the secret conference adjourned after calling for a meeting of the Arab chiefs of staff.

Yolande duly reported on the League's deliberations, but
her dispatches were regarded as not completely reliable. The
Jewish Agency could not believe that the Arabs were determined to violate the U.N. resolution and oppose the major
powers that had voted for the establishment of a Jewish
state. The events of the next few months brought an end to
Yolande's activities. As talk of war increased, new security

measures made it harder for the Haganah agent to obtain information. Her contacts, who in the past had been readily accessible, now demanded higher prices and proceeded with extreme caution. Friends of Yolande, sensing the danger she faced, tried to get her to leave Cairo, but she refused to abandon her mission. She reasoned that the whole apparatus that she had worked so hard to build would crumble without her.

In May, 1948, following Egypt's attack on the Jews in Palestine, Yolande was arrested along with thousands of other Egyptian Jews suspected as Jewish agents and Zionist sympathizers. Her arrest had been delayed for several months thanks to the efforts of friends in key positions. In prison she was accorded special treatment but, nevertheless, her health worsened. Mohi Bey, at the risk of his own life, managed to get her out of jail and took her to Paris where she was appointed to the staff of the Israel U.N. Mission in that city. She derived much satisfaction from her work, but within a short time she was hospitalized and underwent several operations. Throughout her illness Mohi Bey remained a steadfast friend. He had given up his position with the Arab League and devoted himself entirely to Yolande.

Her strong desire to live helped her to recover in some measure, and in 1952, Yolande, her aged mother, and Gilbert emigrated to Israel. It was a time of severe austerity, and conditions in the new state were difficult. But Yolande was optimistic. She spoke no Hebrew, and her existence, which seemed drab in comparison to the excitement and danger of her years in Cairo, weighed heavily on her. Her friends, who were now high-ranking government officials, arranged for her to work in the protocol section of the Foreign Ministry. She gracefully accepted the challenge of her new life, learned Hebrew, made new friends, and seemed to be her old, cheerful self. As the years passed,

however, her health—never very strong—seriously deterio-
rated.

Levi Avrahami, who remained a close friend, recalls that
one day while visiting the Knesset (parliament), Yolande
was greeted by David Ben-Gurion, then premier. People
were amazed to see this gruff man warmly embrace an unknown woman in front of the entire assembly. Yolande was
deeply moved by his gesture. She died at the Hadassah
hospital in Jerusalem in 1957.

Her son Gilbert now lives in Switzerland where he is
employed as an economist at a well-known banking institution. Levi Avrahami has held various diplomatic posts since
his Haganah days. He now lives in Jerusalem and is the
director of the Israel Numismatical Society. Eliahu Sassoon,
one of Israel's leading Arab affairs experts, has served as
his country's ambassador to Turkey, Switzerland, and Italy.
He is currently minister of police.

# ❧ The *Lino*

Ⅰ N THE SPRING OF 1948, ISRAELI AGENTS IN PRAGUE reported that the Czech government had agreed to sell sizable quantities of arms to Syria. A Syrian military delegation quickly concluded negotiations for the purchase of six thousand rifles, eight million rounds of ammunition, a large quantity of hand grenades, and other explosives. The arms and munitions were shipped to Yugoslavia where they were loaded onto a small Italian boat known as the *Lino*. From the port of Fiume the ship was to sail to Beirut. The arms would then be transported by land to Syria.

While in the Adriatic, the *Lino* encountered rough weather, and water entered the engine room. The captain was forced to put in immediately for repairs. The *Lino* anchored at Molfetta, not far from Bari in southern Italy. The cargo, which had been kept dry by canvas coverings, was concealed.

At about the same time a group of three men and one woman met in the Mediterano Hotel in Rome. The men were elegantly dressed but only one was easily recognizable as an Italian. One was an Israeli named Yehuda Arzi. His mission was to expedite in any manner possible the shipment of arms to the soldiers of the Haganah. As every cable from headquarters in Tel Aviv reminded him, he was to accomplish his task as soon as possible. But Arzi needed no reminders. He knew that the situation in Palestine was desperate. Daily young men and women risked their lives to accompany convoys to Jerusalem. They were armed with locally manufactured short-range sten guns. Against them the Arabs enjoyed the advantage of up-to-date rifles and machine guns. For years Arzi had served the Haganah in Europe, America, North Africa, and other places. Somehow he had carried on with never enough time to make advance plans and never enough money to finance his operations adequately.

The Italian of the group was known as Bianco, a former vice-admiral of the Italian navy. He had been recruited after the war by the Palestinian organization responsible for the illegal immigration of European Jewish refugees to Palestine. The work was risky, and Bianco's job was to find Italian captains willing to run the British sea blockade. The ports of Italy were full of Italian ex-navy men who sought commissions and were willing to work for low pay. Bianco helped to choose those men who could be counted on.

Though not a Jew, he had come to regard himself as one of the Haganah, engaged in the struggle to establish and secure the Jewish state. The sight of Jewish refugees helplessly waiting for transportation to Palestine aroused his compassion, and the leaders of the Haganah found that Bianco was ready to serve in any capacity. As a former high-ranking naval officer, he was of invaluable assistance in smoothing the Jewish underground's path over many obstacles. He had many contacts among Italian port officials and would frequently use his influence with them to permit some irregular Haganah activity.

In those days the harbors of Italy were jammed with hundreds of abandoned boats. Most of these vessels were unseaworthy, but here and there a ship that looked like a wreck to the unpracticed eye, was salvageable and could, with the investment of much effort, be made to sail again. Bianco knew the ports of his country intimately and he always knew someone who could tip him off to a serviceable vessel. Getting the ship overhauled was just the beginning, for the Italian authorities had a policy of forbidding these vessels to sail without first passing a stiff inspection. Even then, when the boat had passed inspection and was about to sail with hundreds of passengers, the authorities would often refuse to let the captain leave port. Bianco was extremely successful in selecting wrecked ships and then clearing them with his friends in the admiralty. The Israelis had complete trust in him, and the Italians respected him.

The third man at the Hotel Mediterano was approximately thirty-five years old. His quiet manner gave no indication of the many daring and strategic missions he had carried out for the Haganah. His name was Munya Mardor, and his exploits were already lengendary in the Zionist underground. He was in Rome waiting for a plane to take him to Tel Aviv after having completed a mission elsewhere in Europe. His superiors had decided to take advantage of his presence by asking him to act as a consultant in the assignment at hand. As he sat and listened to the others, his sunburned face revealed no reaction. He hardly spoke, but what he did say was well thought out and carefully considered. He inspired confidence in others, and it was understandable that one of the popular slogans of Haganah operatives was, "We'll follow Munya anywhere."

The woman was Ada Sereni, the widow of Enzo Sereni, the Haganah officer who had parachuted behind German lines in occupied Italy and had been captured and killed. Ada was the daughter of a prominent Italian-Jewish family and she strongly identified with the Zionist cause. She was involved in practically every Haganah activity then going on in Italy: illegal immigration, arms smuggling, recruitment of Italian navy men, and negotiations with government ministers. She had excellent connections, thanks to her family, and her enthusiasm and inexhaustible energy enabled her to accomplish the seemingly impossible. Though she had never been officially appointed chief of Haganah operations in Italy, the force of her personality and her persuasive manner often convinced others to act in accordance with her wishes.

The four sat in the lobby of the hotel and discussed events in Palestine. They were impatiently waiting for an urgent message. Finally the receptionist called out, "Signor Arzi, your call to Geneva."

"Put it through to room 362. I'll be right there."

Arzi lifted the receiver. The thick voice on the other end was that of Shaul Avigour, European commander of the Haganah. His headquarters were in Geneva.

Their talk was guarded, and they avoided the use of names whenever possible. They knew that their conversation might be monitored by pro-Arab Italian elements, and Arzi had already spotted a telephone operator making notes of his calls. After an innocuous greeting and some misleading sentences, Shaul said, "You have to take the girl out to sea as soon as possible. Use Danny's men."

Arzi immediately understood that "girl" meant the *Lino* and that "Danny's men" was a reference to the Israeli airforce men commanded by Danny Agronski who were using Italy as a base for smuggling planes to Palestine. Shaul was telling them to sink the ship from the air.

The airforce men passed themselves off as employees of a Panamanian air-transport company who had been ordered to stop in Italy. A few of them were Americans, former fighter pilots who had volunteered to assist the Jews in Palestine in the struggle against the Arabs. The British were still the official authorities in Palestine, and the flyers could not openly reveal themselves as Israeli pilots.

Even if Agronski were willing to carry out Avigour's order, it would be close to impossible. The pilots flying C-46's had no bomb crews and lacked bombs. Furthermore, they had no idea where they could obtain them in Italy. Even if they could find bombs, they would have trouble getting them onto a plane under the surveillance of Italian airport officials.

Munya Mardor, who was practically a saboteur by profession, was also unhappy with the bombing plan. He reasoned that the main problem was to make sure that no harm came to the *Lino*'s crew or else the Italian government would certainly conduct an intensive investigation. Even if the crew came through unharmed, the markings of the planes would be spotted and the pilots' Panamanian cover would be blown. Mardor was typical of the Haganah officers who had been trained to fight and at the same time respect the sanctity of human life. He was always careful to protect innocent lives.

He decided that the mission as planned could not be accomplished, but since he was not in charge and had only been called in as a consultant, he could only offer his advice. Then, too, he might not be around very long, as he was due to return to Tel Aviv on the first available flight.

In spite of this, Mardor could not detach himself. He worried about complications and possible bloodshed. He knew that if the arms reached the Syrian "Army of Liberation," they could play a decisive role in the fight against the Jews.

There were so many factors to be considered. The Italians were sympathetic to the Israelis. They looked the other way as the Haganah systematically smuggled thousands of refugees into Palestine. The British and the Arabs constantly complained about Haganah activities in Italy, and occasional difficulties notwithstanding, the Italians proved to be valuable allies. Thanks to the friendship of several highly placed government officials, a few quiet arms deals had already been concluded and air travel between Italy and Palestine increased. Italy was crucial to the Jews as a point of departure in Europe. But this assistance would be withdrawn if open acts of sabotage were carried out on Italian soil. If such a breach were to occur, it would be beyond the powers of Bianco and Ada Sereni to repair it.

Mardor tried to work out an alternate plan. He was convinced that if he told Avigour the aerial bombardment scheme was not feasible but that he had devised another plan, the Haganah commander would agree to a change of orders. He spent the day strolling about Rome and contemplating various courses of action. One idea was to meet the *Lino* at sea with an illegal immigrants' boat. He would have a trained group board the Italian ship, overpower the crew, and take the vessel to Tel Aviv. Another possibility was sinking the *Lino* at sea after first transferring the crew to an Israeli ship. But these plans were next to impossible to carry out. He kept pondering the problem.

It was a beautiful day, and as he passed by playing children and strolling couples, the conflict in his country seemed distant and futile. He thought of the Jewish youngsters in Palestine training for war and being exposed to Arab snipers as they guarded convoys up through the Judean Hills to Jerusalem. Newly arrived, young immigrants who had just run the British sea blockade were pressed into service before they had even seen Israel by day or spoken a word of Hebrew. Their equipment was inferior and many of them had never held a gun before.

By the time he returned to the Hotel Mediterano, he had made up his mind. He told Ada of his objections to Shaul Avigour's orders and she agreed. She would have to continue working in Italy and did not want Italian security police harassing her. They decided to call Shaul and inform him of their decision.

Avigour exploded on the phone: "You must take care of the girl at all costs. Israel is bleeding. Any more arms for the Arabs are liable to swing the balance."

Shaul appointed Munya head of the operation and ordered

him to get in touch with Agronski and his men. Munya called them together, and they were joined by Yosele Dror, one of the Haganah's best saboteurs, who had recently been summoned to Italy.

The American pilots were incredulous. "What kind of war is this?" they asked. They were used to bombing German cities, ammunition dumps, and railroad junctions, and they were well acquainted with enemy fighter planes and the danger of antiaircraft fire from the ground. But when bombing such targets, they had pressed a button and that was that. Now it seemed like a bad joke to have to toss primitive bombs out of an airplane with no directional instruments onto a moving ship and at the same time conceal the plane's markings—and then to have to fly back to Italy and land while the suspicious Italians watched them. The further suggestion that they throw the bomb out tied to a rope suspended from the door handle seemed to them sheer insanity. Nevertheless, they were impressed by the air of confident authority Munya exuded and accepted his instructions.

Dror was put in charge of assembling the bombs. He required TNT and other explosive materials. To make matters even more difficult, the Italian election campaign was underway, and there was talk of a Communist conspiracy. All sales of explosives had been prohibited, and warehouses were carefully watched. Yosele looked everywhere. Finally he located an old Haganah laboratory in Milan where he found explosives, detonators, and fuses. His crew worked day and night, and while they were excellent saboteurs—the British mandate authorities in Palestine could verify this—constructing small bombs to be dropped on a moving ship was an extremely difficult task. They did not like the idea of guiding the bomb by tying it to a rope suspended from the plane, because they feared that the aircraft might also be blown up.

Their doubts urged Munya once again to appeal to Avigour in Geneva. He suggested an alternate plan but could not go into detail on the phone. He decided to take full responsibility for the mission and devised another scheme. The Haganah possessed a speedboat in one of the southern ports. All it needed were a few minor repairs. It could easily overtake the *Lino*, and a group of Haganah men could then board the Italian ship and sail her to an Israeli port. If they encountered a British patrol boat, they would sink the *Lino*. A tall, husky, Irish-looking young man named Amnon Yona was selected to head the boarding party.

Bianco was put in charge of readying the speedboat. The repair work on the *Lino* was already finished, and Munya knew that time was running out. He needed several more days for preparations. The orders from Tel Aviv were un-equivocal: "The *Lino* must not arrive at her destination." Ben-Gurion himself had signed one of the cables, a clear indication of the tremendous importance of the mission. Munya asked Ada if there was any way of delaying the *Lino*'s departure from Bari.

Ada approached admirals, cabinet ministers, and other officials and informed them that the *Lino* was a munitions ship transporting arms for a war that was against the wishes of the United Nations. She urged them to search the ship.

In the port of Molfetta, harbor authorities asked the aging captain of the *Lino*, Vizolo Pietro, for his documents. The old man refused, saying that he had only entered the port to make emergency repairs and seek shelter from a storm. He maintained that his cargo was onions. The authorities, however, were insistent, and with Bianco's encouragement port officials carried out a search. Under a shallow layer of onions, crates of rifles were uncovered. The harbor police were furious. The boat's crew was placed under detention, and the *Lino* was docked in the military section of Bari port. The detention order stated that the action was taken because of false declarations concerning the ship's cargo, but Ada and Munya knew that the order would be overruled as soon as the Syrian embassy in Rome began agitating for the immediate release of the ship.

The political tension in Italy on the eve of elections helped Munya and Ada. A nicely managed news leak resulted in banner headlines the next day—"Arms Ship Detained in Molfetta." The right-wing papers accused the Communists of owning the ship. The fact that the arms were of Czech manufacture and that the ship had passed through Yugoslavia tended to support this contention. The Communist press responded by charging that the rightists had planted the ship in order to discredit the Reds.

*Il Messaggèro,* a conservative paper and the unofficial organ of the Christian Democrats, published the following dispatch from Bari in its editions of April 4:

> The ship *Lino,* which had been forced to take shelter in the port of Molfetta because of engine trouble, was searched by harbor police last night and found to be holding a cargo of ammunition, 400 cases of rifles, and a case of explosives instead of her declared cargo.
>
> Several propagandists, including the Communist mayor of Molfetta, Mateo Altumra, claimed that the ship was sent to rightist elements by the English. Communist party followers have asked that the cargo be unloaded. In light of this development, police reinforcements have been sent from Bari to keep peace in the port.

The report added that later fighting had broken out between Communist supporters and rightists.

In inflammatory language, *L'Unita,* the official newspaper of the Communist party, announced:

> Lying propaganda of the government concerning arms ship in Molfetta harbor . . .
>
> Four hundred cases of rifles and thousands of packs of ammunition discovered on the *Lino* . . .
>
> Italian government maneuvering to conceal affair . . .

The article claimed that when Comrade Altumra asked the police about the arms, he had received no answer. The Mayor, *L'Unita* continued, demanded that the arms be unloaded and the police refused, whereupon Altumra appealed to the port director. The Mayor was finally told that no information would be released since the matter was considered a question of national security. *L'Unita* wrote that it was later discovered that the arms were destined for Syria and attacked the government for "deliberately fabricating" the story of Yugoslav arms for Italian Communists.

Charges and countercharges were heatedly exchanged, and Munya's group gained a few days. In Rome the Syrian ambassador addressed a formal protest to the Italian government over the detention of the ship and its crew. He threatened a worsening of relations between Italy and the Arab nations. Pro-Arab elements within the Foreign Ministry and commercial interests joined Arab diplomats in the protest, and the government was humiliated when it came out that the *Lino* had not violated any regulations by putting in at Molfetta for emergency repairs. The government's feeble explanation was that the incident had occurred during a tense election campaign and was thus understandable if also regrettable.

Time was running out and the speedboat was still not ready. After much discussion it was decided to act while the ship was still in the Bari military harbor.

In Rome, Munya met Dror again. Yosele was well known to Mardor, and one of his exploits involving the mining of a ship was studied as a classic exercise in the frogman courses of several countries. Dror, who was tough and confident, regarded as his primary concern the completion of his mission, no matter what danger he placed himself in to achieve it. Munya's approach was different. He always considered the men carrying out an action and their own safety.

Their meeting was brief. They reviewed their tentative

plan and Munya instructed Yosele, who had to transport the explosive to Bari, to take a double supply of gas, oil, and tires for the truck in order to avoid any delays along the way. Yosele chose his demolition crew and drivers. The truck, disguised as an American occupation army truck, bore the sign: DDT—Disinfection Unit. The tank actually contained DDT, but within it was a concealed container in which the explosive had been carefully packed. It was feared that the truck might be stopped and searched by the police because of the pre-election tension between the Communists and right-wing parties.

Munya issued final instructions, sent a last message to Geneva, and obtained a Polish refugee identification card (there were many displaced Poles in Italy at this time) before leaving for Bari.

The plan that had finally been selected was to sink the *Lino* while it was in Bari harbor. They only had two days to accomplish this.

As soon as Yosele Dror arrived in Bari, he examined the approaches to the harbor and spent the entire day walking by the docks and observing the *Lino* from afar. Munya arrived from Rome the following morning after a tense and sleepless night. The two men met in a room at a nearby displaced-persons camp. Yosele presented his final plan of action. He would rent a rowboat and under cover of darkness row out to the *Lino*. Two other members of his crew would swim out to the ship and secure the bomb to the *Lino*'s hull with vises. The entire crew would then row back to the dock and leave immediately by truck for Rome.

There was friction between the two agents. Dror felt that he knew exactly what to do and resented Mardor's detailed instructions. The latter felt that the mission should be carried out differently. He had seen too many actions fail because of hasty planning and felt that his colleague's self-confidence was exaggerated.

The area chosen for the saboteurs to launch their operation had not been thoroughly checked out, but a cursory inspection revealed that it was alive with activity. There was an army camp nearby, and a British destroyer had recently anchored near the *Lino* to supplement the careful watch already maintained by the Italian harbor police.

For the first time Munya began to worry that in spite of their efforts the *Lino*'s cargo might after all reach the Syrians. He took a ruler and spread out a map of the harbor on a table. After deliberating for a few minutes, he turned to Dror. "Yosele," he began, "your plan calls for the demolition team to swim to the *Lino* just before dawn. If so, how will you have enough time to plant the bomb, board the rowboat, and return to the harbor entrance before daybreak? You'd be caught in the middle of the harbor, not far from the army camp."

Yosele's other calculations were also challenged. Taking the boat and rowing around the breakwater depended on maximum speed. Suppose the weather were bad and they couldn't rent a boat. And even if they did find a boat, whoever rented it would be suspicious if he heard an explosion shortly after they left. Even if they succeeded in planting the bomb, Munya was sure they would be seen upon their return. He rejected Dror's plan as incomplete and faulty.

Yosele bristled. As far as he was concerned, Munya was an armchair commander with no real idea of field conditions. "It makes no difference," he replied sharply. "We must complete the mission or else many of our comrades will needlessly die."

The tension between them grew, and Munya felt that he would first have to break Yosele's stubbornness. At the same time he was reluctant to upset a man who in a few hours would set out on a dangerous operation.

In the Haganah, discipline had always been rather informal. Mutual trust, respect, and friendship were what guided relations among the men of the Jewish underground. Nevertheless, Munya felt he had no choice but to assert his authority in order to gain Dror's confidence. Systematically he attacked Yosele's plan, demolishing it point by point. Finally Munya instituted a meticulous equipment check. By displaying attention to small but crucial details such as painting the boat's oars black so that they would not be seen at night, he was able to win Yosele over.

They went back to the map and once again measured distances, studied directions, and made numerous calculations. Suddenly Munya had an idea. "The promenade surrounding the harbor," he exclaimed. "That's where the answer is."

Munya, Yosele, and Amnon Yona circled the harbor promenade in a small Fiat. They were sure that at some point along the walk they would find a suitable launching spot. They left the car and continued their tour on foot. At one point they noticed a cement wall separating the promenade and harbor. They walked along until they discovered an opening in the wall which would allow them to descend directly to the rocks at the edge of the water. This way they could avoid going around the breakwater.

Munya felt that he was now on the right track, but he still lacked a complete picture of the operation. Each phase had to be accurately charted, as it was not only a question of successfully blowing up the *Lino*. The escape had to be carefully plotted lest they leave any traces linking the action to Israeli agents. If this were to happen, the entire Haganah organization in Italy would be compromised. For the last time Yosele and Munya went over the wind directions and studied the areas of the harbor that were illuminated by searchlights.

That evening they made their first attempt. It was a failure. They were almost spotted in the English destroyer's

searchlights, a dog barked, and there was a group of Italians
in a small boat who almost caught them in the act of plac-
ing the bomb. Everything that could possibly go wrong, did.
It was only luck that brought them back to camp safely.

All next day they discussed the British destroyer. As long
as it guarded the approach to the *Lino,* it would be impossible to sink the arms ship. For hours they discussed new
plans that would take them around the destroyer, but to no
avail. Late in the afternoon one of Yosele's men returned
from a walk with startling news: the British ship was leaving the harbor.

That night they again set out in the Fiat and the DDT
truck for the harbor. Amnon Yona and the wife of the displaced-persons camp director went to their lookout station
on the promenade. They posed as lovers out for a stroll.
Munya waited in the car.

At 9:30, Yosele and his crew tied their tools to their
waists, drank some cognac, and oiled their bodies as protec-
tion against the icy harbor water. They made their way to a
rowboat and set out. Just as everything had gone wrong the
night before, now everything went right. The saboteurs went
about their work calmly and efficiently, rowing silently out
to the ship and scaling its side while lugging their makeshift
bomb behind them.

It was not easy for Munya. Inaction brought on torturing
thoughts. Why hadn't they returned? Did his plan contain
some flaw; had he overlooked some minor point that would
cost the men their lives and the Haganah some of its best
operatives?

There had been no shots. That was a good sign, he told
himself. Yosele's men would not give up without fighting.
But what was taking all this time?

The bomb they used was primitive, fashioned out of parts
from an old motorcycle. One part contained TNT; another

section carried the detonators and fuse apparatus. Around the detonator potash was scattered, and next to it was a bottle of sulphuric acid wrapped in newspaper.

The saboteurs overturned the acid. It would eat through the paper and activate the potash, which would in turn set off the detonator. The problem was that it was impossible to time exactly how long it took the acid to eat through the paper since every experiment produced a different result. They figured they had about two hours to get away.

Munya was overjoyed when he saw Yosele and his men scurry up the embankment onto the promenade. The whole operation had taken an hour and a half, but to Munya it had seemed like days. They left immediately and did not learn of their success until they reached Rome. The make-shift bomb had exploded. The *Lino* was on the bottom of Bari harbor, and it was put there with no loss of life.

Munya sent cables to Ben-Gurion and to Haganah headquarters in Tel Aviv. They said, "Mission accomplished."

The *Lino* episode was closed for the time being. But its cargo would trouble the Haganah again.

# ❧ The *"Brigand"*

I N MAY, 1948, THE SYRIAN GENERAL STAFF WAS IN A state of panic and confusion. The first part of the attack on the Jews in Palestine had already been launched, and the volunteer "Liberation Army" under General Fawzi El Kuakji was clamoring for arms. Weapons had been promised from the Syrian army's regular arsenal, but no shipments were received and Kuakji's men went into battle only to be turned back at the Jewish settlement of Mishmar HaEmek in the Jezreel Valley. Despite their superiority in numbers and armaments to the Jewish forces, the Syrian volunteers returned to their country embittered and ready to blame their humiliating defeat on the powers in Damascus because of their failure to come through with the promised weapons.

In Damascus the lack of emergency planning was evident. No one had envisioned the possibility that the *Lino* would be sunk or that Israel would withstand the first attack. For weeks optimistic cables from the Syrian ambassador in Rome had assured the Defense Ministry that the *Lino* was on its way. The detention of the ship in Bari was seen as a minor delay resulting from a misunderstanding with Italian authorities.

While several units of the Syrian army had already invaded Palestine, other regiments were encamped waiting for arms. Defense officials were afraid to admit that they had not seriously prepared for the war and that the need for a contingency reserve of arms had not been foreseen.

There were rumors of betrayal circulating among the army officers. Young colonels spoke of Israeli agents infiltrating the Syrian Defense Ministry. The traditional feud between civilian officials and the military was out in the open.

Meanwhile reports from the front were received. King Abdullah of Jordan demanded that the Syrians change their plan of attack and, instead of scattering their units, use them as reinforcements for the Arab Legion fighting in the Jordan Valley near the Sea of Galilee. The lack of arms kept thousands of troops idle, and army commanders charged the civilian defense officials with incompetence and, worse, sabotage and corruption.

The suspicions of several army officers, aroused by the inept handling of the Czech arms deal—"how did arms paid for in cash to Czechoslovakia end up on an Italian ship detained in Bari more than a month after it was due to arrive in Beirut?"—led the Syrian premier, Mardem Bey, to intervene personally to prevent a revolt in the army.

One of the most vociferous of the young Syrian army officers was Major Fuad Mardem Bey, a cousin of the Premier and an outspoken opponent of the minister of defense whom he charged with sending troops into battle unprepared. Because of his family connections, Fuad had considerable influence on the junior officers.

The Italian government reacted to the sinking of the *Lino* with profuse apologies to Syria and promises of assistance in salvaging the ship's cargo. Italy was anxious to assuage Damascus and avert a threatened break of diplomatic relations. The government suspected the Communists of sinking the *Lino*. One widely accepted explanation was the rightist saboteurs had blown up the vessel in order to prevent the arms from falling into the hands of the Communists. Despite the several versions current, few people knew that Israeli agents were involved in the *Lino* episode.

Mardem Bey decided to take advantage of the possibility of salvaging the arms shipment by ridding himself of his troublesome relative, Major Fuad. Fuad's angry denunciations of the government were grounds for arrest on charges of treason, but the Premier reasoned that his family would be scandalized if he were to imprison his cousin. He also had no desire to make a martyr of the volatile young officer and by so doing fuel the rebellious mood of many junior army men. By arrangement with the Ministry of Defense and the general staff he succeeded in appointing Fuad as Syria's special envoy to Italy responsible for expediting shipment of the salvaged *Lino* cargo and with authority to contract for further arms.

Fuad arrived in Bari and was assured by the salvage company engaged in raising the wreck that within ten days the weapons would be ready for shipment to the Middle East. He was pleased at the prospect of carrying out his mission and welcomed the opportunity to prove his worth. He was sensitive to the jealousy of his contemporaries who were convinced that his promotion to major had come only because of family connections.

At the port he checked several of the salvaged crates and found that a protective coating had protected the rifles from damage by sea water. Some of the cases of explosives were ruined, but the greater part of the cargo was intact. In an optimistic mood, Fuad sent off the following cable to the Syrian minister of defense and the general staff:

> Have succeeded in saving arms from bottom of sea.
> Making efforts ship them immediately.
>
> Maj. Fuad

For some reason, perhaps unguarded enthusiasm, he neglected to send the message in code. He handed it to the hotel reception clerk who gave it to one of the bellboys to carry to the post office. Within a few hours Fuad's plans were known to the Haganah representatives in Italy. His carelessness may have been due to the fact that he never realized that Israelis were involved in the *Lino* sinking. Nor did he imagine that Israeli agents would be stationed in Bari.

With Munya Mardor's return to Israel, Amnon Yona was put in charge of the Haganah's special unit operating in southern Italy. He ordered his men to keep a constant watch on the speed of the salvage operation and the condition of the arms.

It was difficult to operate in Bari. Though the Syrians did not suspect the Israelis, the Italian police, intelligence services, and counterespionage branch were under strict orders to watch every foreigner in Bari. For this reason Israelis who had to be in the port city for illegal immigration activities or military matters were instructed not to stay in any of the local hotels but to make other sleeping arrangements. It was decided to transfer much of the immigration operation to other ports while Bari was considered a "hot" port.

Giovanni Sartini, the head of Italian security in the city, kept his men in a state of alert, as if a foreign army were trying to sabotage Fuad's efforts. He knew what had actually happened to the *Lino* and was determined not to be surprised a second time. Every hotel was requested to report on any Israelis listed in their registers, and the alien affairs section of the police worked overtime to maintain a constant check on every Palestinian Jew in Bari. The area of salvage operations was under a heavy, twenty-four-hour guard. Under these conditions it was impossible to imagine another sabotage attempt, and Yona was disinclined to consider this approach.

It was decided to try to thwart Fuad in a different manner. Haganah headquarters in Tel Aviv dispatched to Italy an agent named Alfred Baker disguised as a free-lance English journalist. Baker traveled on a British passport and upon his arrival checked in at the Hotel Moderno. His instructions were to make contact with Bianco. After a few days in Bari, Baker left for Rome where Bianco was getting friendly with Fuad. The former Italian naval officer had been introduced to the Syrian as the influential friend of many important people in Rome.

In the Italian capital Baker met and soon fell in love with a beautiful blonde Czech student named Yalik. She had recently defected from Czechoslovakia at the urging of her father, a general who had been a confidant of the Czech president, Eduard Beneš. Following the Communist take-over earlier that year, Yalik become a kind of symbol of resistance for refusing to join the Communist students organization. At Prague University she was an honor student in archeology, and when she received an invitation to attend an archeologists conference in Rome, she accepted and took advantage of the opportunity to defect.

Yalik suspected that Baker was more than a journalist and was mystified by his sudden trips all over Italy. When she discovered that Alfred was Jewish, he explained that he was of British origin but had grown up in Palestine. He did not, however, reveal the purpose of his stay in Italy and clung to his cover story.

Gradually Baker acquainted her with Israel's problems and told her of the frenetic arms race going on in the Middle East. Yalik showed great sympathy for the Jews and proved to be a faithful accomplice.

One evening Baker arranged with Bianco to invite Fuad to dinner at a rather elegant restaurant on one of the picturesque hills overlooking Rome. Baker planned to arrive with Yalik and three lovely Italian girls who were employed by Israeli intelligence in various capacities. On this evening their job was to seduce Fuad. By the time Baker arrived with his party, Bianco and the Major had consumed an excellent dinner and many glasses of choice wine. Fuad was in a mellow mood. Things seemed to be going well and he relished thoughts of his triumphant return to Damascus. The Italian girls played their roles skillfully. They danced near Fuad's table and smiled charmingly at Bianco and his guest. But Fuad had noticed Yalik the moment she entered the restaurant and seemed to be interested only in her. It was apparent that the trio of willing beauties so thoughtfully provided by Baker had little success in diverting the Syrian's attention from the Czech girl. The Israeli had not intended his attractive mistress to be part of that evening's operation.

Later, sitting at Bianco's table with Fuad and Yalik, Baker realized that he couldn't make himself obvious by forcing one of the Italian girls on Fuad, nor could he risk offending the Syrian by taking Yalik away. Too much depended on ingratiating himself with the Major. The Haganah was convinced that through Fuad it could learn a great deal about Syria's plans for arms acquisitions in Europe.

At 2 A.M., Fuad, visibly drunk, stood up and clumsily grabbed Yalik. She cleverly managed to slip out of his hold by promising to visit him at his hotel the next day. When Fuad said goodnight to Bianco, he felt that he had found a friend who would be of immeasurable assistance in dealing with Italian officials. Bianco assured the Arab that he was ready to smooth his way in any matter and even offered to accompany him to Bari the next day to check on the progress of the *Lino* salvage operation. Bianco had already found out that Fuad planned to load the arms on the *Khedive Ismail,* an Egyptian boat scheduled to dock at Genoa at the end of the month.

Israeli intelligence immediately set out to thwart this plan. Ada Sereni was able to use her connections to advantage, and when Fuad applied to the appropriate government offices for permission to load the arms on trucks at Bari and then ship them overland to Genoa, he was refused. The excuse given was that the partially damaged munitions might explode in some urban center.

Fuad soon thought of an alternative plan. The arms would be loaded onto a small Italian boat in Bari and then transported to the Straits of Messina off the Mediterranean where the cargo would be transferred to the *Khedive Ismail*. Several Italian companies sought to undertake the transfer and began submitting bids to the Major. A Syrian businessman living in Italy named Mamduah Al Chafer called Fuad daily and each time offered a cheaper price. Bianco saw that it would be necessary to get around Al Chafer, who actually had excellent connections in Italy and whose price was low. The companies Al Chafer proposed to work with were well known and enjoyed a good reputation with the Syrian legation in Rome.

Bianco got in touch with Giovanni Manara, a friend of his who owned a small boat. They agreed on a fair price for transporting the arms from Bari to Messina, and the commission for the transaction was forwarded to Fuad's bank account. Fuad agreed to Bianco's arrangement and was glad to have the money.

By this time Fuad had lost interest in Yalik and had begun an affair with a beautiful Yugoslav woman named Geri Pelma. Although she posed as a journalist, Geri was known to Rome's elite as an elegant courtesan, possessing great charm and expensive tastes. Baker and Yalik were delighted by this development because it meant that the Czech girl would no longer have to sleep with the Syrian and that Alfred and Bianco could now gain easy access to Fuad's official correspondence. They could rely upon Geri to keep them informed, and she never asked too many questions, such as whom they were working for. Being paid to supply information was not an unusual experience for her in postwar Rome.

Experienced and clever, Geri Pelma had soon captivated Fuad, who was thrilled by the exquisite entertainments she devised for him. Nothing in his experience as a rather libertine army officer matched the subtlety and sensual pleasures of the banquets and orgies at Geri's house. He soon moved in with her and, except for the enormous bills he was frequently presented with, was quite content.

Bianco spent most of his time with Fuad and was able to feed Baker with a constant stream of information regarding Syrian arms purchases in Italy and elsewhere in Europe.

One day two childhood friends of Fuad who had recently arrived in Rome as Syrian agents told the Major that he would have to leave Geri. The agents, Fara As Said and Abd Wazir, claimed that Geri was an expensive prostitute who worked for the Israelis and only pretended to love the Syrian officer.

Enraged, Fuad rushed back to the apartment and confronted Geri. "Do you know any Israelis?" he challenged. "Give me a straight answer."

His outburst was not completely unexpected, for Geri had anticipated just such a scene. Calmly she replied that no Israelis came to her house but that occasionally she met some at parties and receptions. She did not know that Alfred Baker was an Israeli and believed him to be British.

She gently fondled Fuad and kissed him, whispering, "Fuad, my love. These people interfering are jealous of our love. They have never experienced this feeling. What do we care about foolish gossip?" Soon they were in bed making love. Afterward, when the Arab's rage and passion were spent, Geri told him that one night while Fuad was in Bari, As Said had called at the apartment and tried to force himself on her. Only the threat to call the police, she said, had gotten rid of him.

Once again Fuad felt rage welling up inside of him. He would kill As Said, strangle him with his own hands. Geri begged him not to cause a public scandal, and finally Fuad agreed that the best thing would be to avoid completely any future contact with his two jealous countrymen.

The expenses he incurred living with Geri forced Fuad to seek extra sources of income. He exploited his purchasing authority for arms by arranging deals with Al Chafer and then demanding payment from the merchant. Al Chafer decided to expose Fuad's corruption and flew to Damascus where he denounced him in front of the Ministry of Defense. He also told the Syrians of Fuad's failure to arrange for the overland transfer of the salvaged *Lino* cargo from Bari to Genoa. Fortunately for Fuad, Mardem Bey, who had since been replaced as premier, still wielded considerable influence in the Syrian capital. He reminded the defense officials that Fuad was responsible for salvaging sunken arms, and in this way he was able to soften the impact of Al Chafer's denunciation. Nevertheless, the businessman returned to Rome with an official government letter ordering Fuad to consult Al Chafer in all matters pertaining to arms shipments. The letter also stated that Al Chafer was regarded by the Syrian government as having the best connections with the weapons market in Italy and that the funds Fuad was authorized to disburse were to be spent in consultation with the merchant.

When they met after Al Chafer's return to Rome, Fuad and the businessman angrily exchanged accusations. The Major said that he had already arranged with an Italian company to transport the *Lino*'s arms by boat from Bari to Messina for eight million lira.

Al Chafer fumed. He reminded Fuad that he had recommended a company willing to do it for two million lira.

The Major refused to change the arrangement. He charged the merchant with having gone to Damascus just to undermine his mission and smear his name. "You're only interested in profiteering at the expense of the Syrian army," Fuad shouted.

"And you," the enraged businessman retorted, "you are living a sordid, dissolute life and spending a fortune on prostitutes with army funds. You'll pay for this treason."

Fuad was upset and angry. He called Bianco and they met in the comfortable bar of the luxurious Hotel Flore on Via Veneto. The Italian tried to soothe Fuad by suggesting that the merchant might be serving foreign interests, perhaps even enemies of Syria. The Syrian was quick to agree with Bianco's assessment of the situation.

"Of course," he said. "Al Chafer is a foreign agent. Maybe he's even working for the Israelis. I must inform Damascus so that they can take the necessary precautions."

With Bianco he drafted a cable.

> Everything going smoothly. Tomorrow arms to be loaded on *Argiro*. Ship belonging to Manara Line will sail from Bari to Messina for transfer to Egyptian ship *Khedive Ismail*. Have succeeded in salvaging most weapons. Rifles intact, ammunition and explosives only partially damaged. According to sources here, Al Chafer is enemy agent. Take appropriate measures. Greetings to our glorious army.
>
> Maj. Fuad

Bianco took leave of Fuad and said they would meet later for dinner. He immediately informed Amnon Yona of the Syrian's plans.

Later that evening the Italian suggested to Fuad that he move out of Geri Pelma's apartment, as his style of life had attracted the attention of Arab diplomats in Rome and it would be best to avoid any scandal. Meanwhile the Egyptian embassy had telephoned Fuad and warned him that Israeli agents were trying to divert the *Lino*'s cargo. Bianco was able to persuade Fuad that this warning was inspired by Al Chafer and was merely another attempt to discredit the Major.

Bianco had won the confidence of Fuad to the point where the Syrian was content to let his friend oversee the transfer of the arms. Fuad spent the rest of the week with Geri visiting weapons factories during the day and nightclubs in the evenings.

In Bari, Bianco arranged for his own men to sign on the *Argiro* as chief engineer and assistant engineer. They were both instructed to take orders only from Bianco. The captain was in poor health and frequently turned the ship over to his chief engineer while he retired to his cabin. Shortly before the *Argiro* was about to depart from Bari, Bianco told the captain that there had been a change in plans and their destination would be Beirut. The captain protested that they lacked sufficient radio equipment for a voyage of that length, but Bianco quieted him by assuring him that another ship with a radioman and all the necessary equipment would catch up with the *Argiro*. He told the captain that it was impossible to delay any longer.

A few minutes after the *Argiro* sailed out of Bari harbor, a seagram with the following message was sent to the *Khedive Ismail*:

Cancelling Messina arrangements.
Fuad

The Haganah informed Levi Eshkol, who at that time was director-general of the Defense Ministry, that the *Argiro* was at sea.

Bianco had instructed the chief engineer and his assistant to slow down just outside of Italian territorial waters under the pretext of engine trouble and wait for the approach of a fishing boat. Aboard would be two men who would introduce themselves as Egyptians assigned to accompany the arms shipment. One would be a naval officer, the other a radio operator. They would supposedly keep in touch with Beirut and the port of Alexandria, Egypt.

Within a few hours after slowing down, a fishing boat approached the *Argiro,* and two Haganah agents boarded the Italian vessel. They went to the captain and told him that they were Egyptian naval men whom Bianco had assigned to the ship with Fuad's approval. They ordered the captain to change course and head for Alexandria and explained that an Egyptian warship would meet the *Argiro* just outside Egyptian waters. The captain was too ill and tired to protest or ask questions. He noticed that the two men were armed and resolved to make the best of the situation by breaking out a bottle of Chianti and inviting his newest crew members to drink with him.

After setting up their radio equipment, the two Israelis radioed Amnon Yona that they had taken control of the *"Brigand"* (the code name for the *Argiro*) without any fighting and that the fishing boat was on its way back to Italy.

A few hours later Yona received a cable from Levi Eshkol asking for detailed information on the position and speed of the *"Brigand."* He said they could send two boats to one of the Dodecanese Islands in Greece to meet the *"Brigand"* and transfer the cargo to Israeli ships that were already in that vicinity.

Yona answered that Eshkol would be contacted directly by radio from the *"Brigand,"* adding that they had documents in their possession proving Arab violation of a United Nations truce in effect in Palestine at that time. It stipulated that no arms were to be brought in by the warring parties from outside.

The next day, as the *Argiro* approached the Dodecanese

Islands, Eshkol received the following radio message from the Haganah men aboard:

> The captain and crew think we are Egyptians helping them bring the ship to Alexandria. If we decide to transfer the arms to another boat at the Dodecanese Islands, we may have to use force. Suggest we approach shores of Israel and then confiscate the cargo on the grounds that it is a violation of U.N. embargo. We can prove real destination of arms, so we have some basis for this excuse. It is essential that the crew be kept in ignorance until the last possible moment. Another possibility is that we sail directly to Haifa while deceiving the captain into thinking that we are coming into Beirut until the last minute. Either of these plans is preferable to an incident in the Greek Islands.

The two Israelis on the *Argiro* waited impatiently for a reply, but Eshkol refused to issue any final orders. He merely radioed them to slow down and report their position every four hours.

Another day passed without final orders. Aboard the *Argiro* they began to worry that Egyptian warships might be following them to accompany the cargo to Alexandria. They radioed Eshkol to consider this possibility and begged him for final orders.

At that moment two Israeli naval ships were in the vicinity of the *Argiro*, but because they feared the presence of Egyptian ships, they refrained from announcing their position.

Fuad expected the *Argiro* to arrive in Alexandria on the morning of August 28. He flew ahead to prepare a reception. The Syrian ambassador, the military attaché and other senior embassy officials were due to take the train from Cairo to Alexandria where the Major had arranged to set up a festive banquet to celebrate the arrival of the weapons.

The morning and afternoon passed, and there was no

word from the *Argiro*. The embassy people began sipping aperitifs and dining without Fuad, who frantically called the port every few minutes to find out if the *Argiro* had been sighted. He explained to the Syrian ambassador that he had cut costs by having the *Argiro* sail directly to Alexandria rather than transfer the arms to the *Khedive Ismail* in Messina. The Egyptian ship had arrived the day before, and this fact only served to aggravate the situation. By midnight Fuad was desperate. He cabled Bianco but received no reply from Italy.

The next day Damascus ordered Fuad to have the embassy in Rome look into the matter. Fuad was frightened. All he needed now was for his enemies in Italy, namely Al Chafer, to find out that something had gone wrong.

"Perhaps the ship had some engine trouble," he feebly tried to explain. Another day went by without any information, and the Major was on the verge of a nervous breakdown. He thought of calling out Egyptian planes and warships. Damascus kept asking him when the ship would arrive, and to make matters worse he received congratulations from some of his friends who wrote that it was good to see how a young, energetic officer could handle things better than civilians.

Fuad flew back to Rome where Geri Pelma was waiting for him. She knew how to soothe the distraught Arab, and the next two days were spent drinking and carousing in her apartment. Bianco turned up in his usual cheerful mood with a seagram announcing that the *Argiro* had had a slight accident near the Dodecanese Islands and would soon be on its way.

The "slight accident" of Bianco's report was actually the sinking of the *Argiro* after its cargo and crew had been transferred to two Israeli ships. Two days later the ships entered the Haifa port, and the arms were sent immediately to Israeli army units.

The Italian captain and his crew were arrested and kept in comfortable quarters at a kibbutz. It was decided that it would be best to delay their return to Italy for a while to avoid complications until the affair blew over. It was also thought that it would be best to keep Fuad in the dark as long as possible. Unfortunately, the captain died from advanced tuberculosis while at the kibbutz, and it was decided to release the crewmen after they had signed affidavits that they had been well treated and that the captain had died a natural death.

Fuad, believing Bianco's story, rushed back to Damascus to explain to the government. He was arrested on arrival. The government had already found out what had happened to the *Argiro*.

Fuad was put on trial for treason the following year. The prosecution charged that a Czech-Jewish beauty in Rome had persuaded the Major to hand over to Israel eight thousand rifles and a million rounds of ammunition that were destined for Syria. It was further alleged that the arms had been purchased from Czechoslovakia and had been shipped to Italy on a ship whose captain was a Communist who planned to deliver the arms to the Italian Communists on the eve of the national elections. The trial sought to discredit several members of former Premier Mardem Bey's regime, but in Fuad's case the distortions made little difference, for the truth would not have helped him. The court was also treated to an explicit description of Fuad's life in Rome with Geri Pelma. Conclusive evidence at the trial was a written statement by the Italian crew of the *Argiro* explaining exactly what had happened.

Although the death penalty was asked, the Major was sentenced to a long prison term. From his prison cell Fuad wrote many letters to Geri Pelma. He never received an answer.

PART II

# ⚜ Between War and Peace

THE ARMISTICE AGREEMENTS SIGNED BY ISRAEL AND the Arab nations in 1949 were viewed hopefully by many Israelis as the prelude to permanent peace treaties. Unfortunately, this hope was to be disappointed. Hostility toward Israel continued unabated. Out of the internal political and social convulsions which took place in many Arab states there emerged new leaders who saw in the Palestine issue a useful means of diverting attention from the shortcomings of their respective regimes. Incitements to take vengence on the "Zionists" who had "usurped" Arab land became a permanent feature of Arab propaganda and led to a policy of continually harassing Israel.

One method of harassment favored by Egypt, and to some extent by Syria, was the infiltration of Israel's borders by operatives who sought information on Israel's military preparedness. The intruders were frequently caught by the alert Israeli border patrol and interrogated.

These interrogations yielded a picture of Egyptian intelligence as a rather perfunctory activity involved in collating Israeli newspaper and press reports. Captured Egyptian documents of that period reveal a fairly low level of competence.

In addition to espionage, robbery and smuggling—particularly narcotics—were the usual motives behind border infiltration. The infiltrators from Egypt would usually cross over in the vicinity of the Gaza Strip on Israel's southern border. The strip was under Egyptian administration and contained several Palestinian refugee camps supported by the United Nations Relief Works Agency. The operatives would spend a few days talking with Arab bedouins in the Negev, gather whatever newspapers were available, and then make their way back to their bases in the Strip.

But with the advent of the Free Officers' *coup d'état* in Egypt in 1954 and the rise to power of Gamal Abdel Nasser, the Egyptian secret service was transformed into a professionally run, aggressive agency.

Nasser's propaganda officials launched a radio war directed against Israel and aimed at promoting pro-Nasser sentiment among Israel's indigenous Arab population. The broadcasts consisted of violent harangues against the "Zionists" and called for the annihilation of Israel and the liberation of Palestine. This approach had some success, as evidenced by the scores of young Israeli Arabs who began fleeing across Israel's borders to neighboring Arab countries.

While some crossed to Jordan or Lebanon in search of a better life and the opportunity of living within a dominant Arab culture, many youths who made their way to the Gaza Strip wanted to join the Egyptian campaign against Israel. Gaza had nothing else to offer. It was an area of grinding poverty and squalid refugee settlements.

Many of the Palestinian Arabs recruited by Egypt were trained as terrorist commandos known as Fedayeen, or "those who sacrifice themselves." Fedayeen units carried out attacks on Israeli border settlements and also guided espionage agents to the frontier. The agents would concern themselves with surveillance and intelligence gathering and leave sabotage to the Fedayeen, who occasionally extended their forays well beyond the borders and struck installations and civilian dwellings close to urban centers.

Between 1949 and 1956 about 1,300 Israelis were killed and wounded by Fedayeen attacks.

Egyptian infiltration intelligence operations gathered information on Israel's defense situation by observing troop training and deployment in the Negev region, photographing defense installations, charting roads, and sketching bridges and other strategic points. Often bedouins were recruited and paid to carry out these missions. Bedouins riding their camels close to military areas were often stopped and found to be in the possession of sophisticated cameras. The bedouins were used extensively because they knew Israel well and were able to spy without arousing suspicion. The Israeli Arabs serving Egyptian intelligence were difficult to identify since they carried valid Israeli identification cards and were accorded assistance by the largely sympathetic Arab minority.

Israeli counterespionage forces waged a daily struggle against the infiltrators. Hundreds of enemy agents were arrested every year. The newspapers frequently carried reports of ambushes and armed clashes involving infiltrators near the borders.

By 1960, Egypt's espionage network had developed into an apparatus of considerable scope. No longer did it have to depend on the routine collation of newspapers for its information. It had succeeded in thoroughly penetrating the Arab communities of Israel where it had established permanent contacts, espionage cells, secret rendezvous points, and password and code systems for relaying instructions and information across the border. Syria had also begun stepping up its spying operations.

The Arab secret services began employing agents from among foreign journalists, United Nations Truce Supervision Organization personnel, and international businessmen. They were also able to make use of deserters from the Israeli army.

The pro-Arab policy of the Communist bloc countries also aided Arab espionage agencies and placed at their disposal the sophisticated training methods of the Soviet Union and other East European intelligence services.

The next four chapters tell the stories of four spies captured in Israel as a result of counterespionage efforts.

# ❦  Mary Frances Hagen

VEN AS A YOUNG GIRL MARY FRANCES HAGEN DIS-
played a fascination with the foreign and exotic. She was
intellectually curious and highly romantic, a combination
that caused her to seek adventures that were beyond the
ken of most American women of her prosperous and con-
ventional background.

Her parents sent her to a reputable college in New
England and probably anticipated a proper marriage and
decent family for their daughter. But Mary was different.
She could not be like other girls her age and had little
interest in their pursuits. At college she ignored the dances
and parties of campus life and spent much of her time in
isolation.

One day after her graduation from college Mary visited
United Nations headquarters in New York City. She was
deeply impressed by the imposing façade of the world
organization and especially by the many dignified and
handsome diplomats she saw in the General Assembly hall
and Secretariat building. The scene at the U.N. fed her
imagination. She had fantasies of belonging to this international world of important political events, famous
statesmen, travel, and intrigue. The U.N. to Mary meant
excitement and romance, and she resolved to move to
New York and seek a job as a correspondent. But she was
soon disappointed. She discovered that few American news-

papers maintain staff U.N. reporters and that those large papers and news services with bureaus at the world organization had no use for a fledgling journalist like Mary.

Nevertheless, Mary decided to stay on in New York and began spending her days in the delegates lounge. It was not difficult to gain entry as security is only stringent during General Assembly sessions and other important meetings. Gradually she became acquainted with several delegates and foreign correspondents. After a while she began to think of herself as a member of the international community. Eventually her contacts led to odd jobs for various delegations. Someone would want a letter or memo typed or something written in idiomatic English; another diplomat would need help in finding an apartment or arranging some other personal matter. Mary proved adept at all these tasks and she soon became the favorite of the Syrian delegation. She helped the delegates write speeches in English, carried out research, and assisted in several other areas.

She was fond of the Arabs she met at the U.N. Their courtly manners and exotic looks pleased her and filled her with romantic notions. The Syrians grew to trust her, and she repaid their confidence by devotion and dedication to the Arab cause. She familiarized herself with Arab arguments and propaganda and became an apologist for their cause. She wrote letters to various publications and gave lectures on the Middle East and the Arab-Israeli dispute.

Mary was particularly attracted to Galab Alchieli, the deputy head of the Syrian delegation. They were two opposites drawn to each other. Galab was recalled to Damascus. His superiors warned him that his relations with Mary would jeopardize his career. Galab argued that Mary had been a great help to him and was devoted to the Arab cause. His colleagues tried to persuade him to forget her and cited other Syrians who had ruined promising careers because of entanglements with foreign women. Galab insisted that he loved Mary and that he was convinced of her devotion and trustworthiness.

In New York, Mary waited for word from Galab. Before he left, they had agreed that he would make all the necessary arrangements to be married. She decided to go to Syria on her own and find out what had happened. When she arrived, she was treated suspiciously. Galab had recently been appointed head of the American desk in the Syrian Foreign Ministry and was told that marriage to a foreigner violated the regulations of diplomatic service and constituted a security risk. He attempted to appeal the case and sought an interview with Serraj A-Din, the chief of Syrian intelligence, to try to convince him of Mary's loyalty to the Arabs. He told A-Din of Mary's activities in New York and of how much she hated Israel.

A-Din, who was later to become the ruthless and dictatorial head of a revolutionary junta, was amused by Galab's earnestness.

"If you're so sure of your girlfriend's reliability, let's test her," he suggested. "With press credentials she can enter Israel without difficulty. We'll instruct her in matters of interest to us. She'll use Tel Aviv as the base of her operations. The Israel press office will no doubt arrange trips to border areas for her as it does for other correspondents. She will be able to photograph and report on fortified border settlements."

There are several versions of the way Galab reacted to A-Din's proposal. Some Israeli intelligence agents claim that Galab agreed to send Mary on this dangerous mission because of patriotic reasons. Other sources maintain that Galab was shocked by the idea and refused to consider it but that Mary, after some deliberation, decided to accept the challenge in order to prove her loyalty and in this way gain permission to marry Galab.

However it came about, Mary was given some training as a Syrian agent. She flew to Israel by way of Cyprus and registered as a foreign correspondent. She began a systematic study of the country, obtained maps, and toured extensively.

It was 1956, several months before the Sinai Campaign, and the situation along Israel's borders had become intolerable. Egyptian terrorist Fedayeen units made daily raids on frontier kibbutzim, killing settlers and destroying property.

Finally, in October, 1956, after Egypt blocked the Gulf of Aqaba, closing the way to Israel's port of Eilat, Israel attacked in a preventative action and drove the Egyptian army out of the Sinai Peninsula. The Fedayeen bases in Gaza and Sinai were destroyed. Israel's offensive was launched in concert with France and Britain, who were concerned over the future of the Suez Canal, and captured the area controlling the international waterway. But the border security gained by Israel in the Suez Campaign was short-lived. The United Nations and the United States brought pressure on Jerusalem to withdraw from the Sinai in return for meaningless guarantees that Israel would be allowed to use the Suez Canal. Special U.N. emergency forces were stationed along the Sinai borders and the Gaza Strip where an uneasy truce prevailed until May, 1967, when Secretary General U Thant acceded to Nasser's demand that the U.N. forces be withdrawn, thus precipitating the Six-Day War.

Mary Hagen's espionage in the first half of 1956 concerned the Syrian border where a narrow strip of territory separated the two countries. Although this territory was a demilitarized zone, every day Israeli farmers cultivating

*Yolande Hermor,*
*Israel's woman in Cairo.*

*Eliahu Sassoon, Israel's*
*special envoy to the Arabs*
*during the pre-1948*
*struggle for the*
*Jewish State.*

*Levi Avrahami, head of*
*Haganah intelligence in*
*Egypt during and after*
*World War II.*

*The* Lino *and its cargo of Arab arms sinking in Bari harbor.*

*Munya Mardor, one of the Haganah's leading sabotage experts.*

*Ada Sereni, key Haganah
agent in Italy.*

*Mary Frances Hagen*

*Yoakim Al Antoni, Coptic
priest and Arab spy.*

*Achmed Utman, member of Egyptian intelligence.*

*Kobruk Yaakovian, Egypt's "Lone Wolf" spy.*

*Eli Cohen, Israeli spy in Damascus.*

*Wolfgang Lotz at his riding academy in suburban Cairo.*
(BLACK . STAR)

*Eli Cohen hanging in the Martyrs' Place, Damascus, May 1965.*

*Isser Harel, former chief of the Central Intelligence and Security Agency.*

*General Aaron Yariv, chief of Israeli Military Intelligence.*

*A section of Israel's national water carrier in the Galilee.
Syria's hydraulic diversion scheme sought to prevent the Israeli
irrigation project.* (ISRAEL INFORMATION SERVICES)

*A destroyed Syrian tank installation in the Golan Heights.*
(ISRAEL INFORMATION SERVICES)

*Up-to-the-minute intelligence enabled Israeli jets to destroy*
*Egypt's entire air force on the first morning of the Six-Day War,*
*June 1967.* (ISRAEL INFORMATION SERVICES)

their lands in the area were killed by Syrian fire from the heights overlooking the string of Jewish Valley settlements.

Despite the presence of long-range Soviet cannons in the Golan Heights overlooking Israel, the Syrians knew that Israeli forces were stationed at well-concealed locations throughout the north and that these units were capable of striking back at Syria. Mary Hagen's assignment was to find out as much as possible about Israeli troop deployment in the border area.

Though she kept up her journalist cover, Mary began to attract the attention of Israel's counterespionage agents by her unusual inquisitiveness. She regularly requested permission to tour the demilitarized zone and always tried to visit the scene of the frequent border incidents immediately after they occurred. Her questions indicated a thorough Arab indoctrination, while this in itself was not suspect—pro-Arab correspondents were not exceptional in Israel—her propensity for taking pictures in areas of the demilitarized zone directly in the line of Syrian fire roused suspicion.

Israeli intelligence decided to detain her for interrogation discovered that she possessed notebooks containing classified military information, as well as maps and pictures of strategic installations and military convoys. She also had political material that had been requested by Syrian intelligence.

She was tried *in camera* for security reasons and convicted on August 27, 1956, of spying for an enemy nation. She confessed to most of the charges and told the story of her engagement to Galab. She maintained that her deep conviction of the justice of the Arab cause had led her to spy for Syria.

The instructions she had received were similar to the ones given to scores of infiltrators, Palestinian Arabs, and smugglers, and it was evident that Syrian intelligence did not consider her one of their prize agents. In a sense, Mary Hagen was a "throw-away" spy—whatever intelligence she produced was welcome but her failure cost the Syrians nothing in terms of compromising their operations.

Mary was sentenced to fifteen months' imprisonment, more in the way of a warning than a punishment. She was released on April 20, 1957, after serving only eight months of her sentence, thanks to the intervention of her family and the United States State Department who promised that she would not return to Syria.

Once back in New York she contacted Galab, who was in Damascus, and was bitterly disappointed by his reaction. In desperation, Mary tried to leave for Damascus to see Galab but her passport was taken away.

Shortly after his appointment as head of the Syrian Broadcasting Service, Galab hired Mary as the Radio Damascus correspondent at the U.N. She was paid well and Galab saw to it that her dispatches were used regularly.

Unfortunately the job did not last long, as Mary soon fell victim to one of Syria's frequent political intrigues. At the General Assembly session which Mary covered for Radio Damascus for the first time, several high-ranking Syrians, including the Baath party leader and foreign minister, Salah Al Bitar, arrived at the U.N. Members of the entourage sought to discredit certain members of the regime by pointing out to Al Bitar that Mary lacked the necessary qualifications to be a correspondent for the Syrian Broadcasting Service. Al Bitar ordered the minister of information to fire her, and Galab protested. But he was helpless, and the minister, who was under heavy pressure, finally dismissed Mary. The affair, which had become a political football, was exploited by several Syrian newspapers.

Mary stayed on at the United Nations and was eventually hired to run the U.N. bureau of McGraw-Hill World

News, the news-gathering organization for McGraw-Hill business periodicals.

Her experience in Israel had one positive result. A few years ago, Judge Chaim Cohen, one of Israel's leading jurists, was touring the world studying various penal systems prior to instituting reforms within Israel's system. At the United Nations he visited the officials of several agencies and was surprised when Mary Hagen requested an interview. He agreed to meet her and she presented him with a number of complaints about her treatment at Neve Tirza women's prison in Israel. Her remarks and suggestions were embodied in Cohen's final report.

# ❦ Yoakim Al Antoni

As the head of the coptic church in israel, Yoakim Al Antoni was a well-known and highly regarded figure. Although the adherents of the ancient Christian sect in Israel were relatively few in number, the government valued Al Antoni's cooperation and goodwill. Israel pursued a policy of safeguarding religious and cultural freedom for the Moslem and Christian minorities in the country. The case of the Coptic Church was special, as Israeli officials felt that since the Copts in Egypt were being persecuted, their coreligionists in Israel would certainly be loyal to Egypt's number-one enemy. The special attitude toward Al Antoni was based on the maxim: "the enemy of my enemy is my friend."

The priest was permitted to cross the border between Israel and Jordan at will and was accorded diplomatic status, which meant that he was not searched or questioned.

Al Antoni's residence was in Jaffa, the ancient city adjacent to Tel Aviv on Israel's Mediterranean coast. He lived near the ornate Coptic Church surrounded by a high stone wall. On Sundays the church would fill with the faithful who attended services and also held their weddings and christenings there. Al Antoni officiated at all ceremonies and was on intimate terms with his congregants. He knew details of their lives and problems and was frequently consulted on both spiritual and practical matters.

During the week the running of the church was left to a young assistant as Al Antoni visited Coptic communities throughout Israel. His followers were Arabs who had elected to remain in Israel after the 1948 war. Regularly the Coptic patriarch stopped in Haifa, Nazareth, Jerusalem and visited villages in Arab areas. He genuinely seemed to enjoy traveling about, and although his congregants suggested that they could easily save him the trouble of a journey by coming to Jaffa for religious ceremonies, Al Antoni continued to tour Coptic communities regularly, no matter how small or how far from Jaffa. He was an accessible, garrulous cleric, always interested in the latest news of each village. He seemed to like being *au courant* with whatever was happening in the country.

Perhaps if Yoakim Al Antoni had been more careful, he would never have been caught. But the ease with which he was able to cross the border to rendezvous with Egyptian intelligence liaison agents in Jordan and the obvious respect shown to him at the Mandelbaum Gate checkpoint caused him to become overconfident. He was convinced that the Israeli authorities would never dare infringe on his status and would never doubt that his trips to Jordan had any other purpose than administration of Coptic affairs in both countries.

One winter morning in 1957, as the Coptic priest drove up through the Judean Hills to Jerusalem, Abba Manilewitz, an Israeli customs officer, arrived at his post in the Mandelbaum Gate's green customs shed. Inside, Sergeant Malka of the Israeli police was studying some papers at his desk. Manilewitz had just settled down at his desk when an automobile from the Israeli side of Jerusalem pulled up at the shed. Manilewitz immediately recognized the bearded, round face of Al Antoni behind the wheel. The priest held a small briefcase, and a larger case was carried by his aide seated next to him.

The customs officer recalled that he had recently received a memo about the priest. He dimly remembered that it had something to do with a switch to different duties. He dug the memo out of a file in his desk and read that Al Antoni, head of the Coptic Church in Israel for the last sixteen years, had recently been assigned to head the Coptic Church in Jordan. Manilewitz also recalled that the last time the priest had entered Israel from Jordan he said he would be staying for a month and a half. It seemed to the customs inspector that Al Antoni was returning before the specified time. Manilewitz hesitated before asking to see the priest's luggage. The Coptic leader enjoyed a status similar to diplomats and U.N. personnel, but a vague suspicion overcame his hesitation and he asked to see Al Antoni's briefcase.

"Why all of a sudden?" the priest asked, barely concealing his annoyance.

"Just a routine inspection," Manilewitz answered in an even tone.

Al Antoni picked up the briefcase and tried to lock it, but the Israeli stopped him and asked if he had anything to declare.

"No, nothing," the priest replied nervously.

Saying to himself, "If they haven't caught him with anything these past fifteen years, what's the point of investigating him this morning," Manilewitz was about to mark the briefcase with chalk indicating that it had cleared customs. But once again a premonition moved him to check the briefcase. He felt the bottom and lifted out three Israeli yearbooks and several papers filled with Arabic writings. He asked what was written on the papers and without waiting for an answer continued his search. Antoni tried to conceal some other papers in his briefcase, but Manilewitz took them from him, saying that they would be returned with the rest of his documents.

The priest's behavior and the suspicious nature of the

papers he was carrying prompted the customs inspector to seek instructions from Sergeant Malka.

"Search all of his belongings," was Malka's terse order.

Al Antoni started to shout, "What's the matter? All of a sudden you don't trust me? The president of Israel, the minister of religion, they will bear witness to my loyalty. Call them. They will tell you who Al Antoni is."

Suddenly he lunged at Manilewitz's table, grabbed the papers, and ran into the toilet, locking the door behind him. The customs inspector was dumbfounded by the priest's unexpected behavior. A few minutes later Al Antoni emerged from the toilet muttering in Hebrew and Arabic, "Enough, I don't want to go to Jordan now. I'm going home." The papers he had snatched were gone, but floating in the toilet bowl were traces of the documents he had flushed down.

After thoroughly searching his robes and belongings, the Israelis found a small piece of paper hidden under Al Antoni's photograph on his identification card. It contained a cipher written in green ink. Additional notes in Arabic were found.

The priest was enraged, but the evidence was incriminating. He was turned over to the counterespionage service and interrogated five times that day. He steadfastly denied everything and claimed that he was taking the yearbooks to the Coptic seminary in Jordanian Jerusalem at the request of the principal. He had broken no law in purchasing the yearbooks since they had been published and contained no classified information. But the papers bearing lists of Israeli airfields, munitions factories, army camps, and other defense installations were another matter. All of these data were classified. The Coptic leader claimed that he was writing a book about Israel and had been gathering material for the last twenty years. He denied that he had been spying against the country and swore that he was a loyal citizen who frequently worked in Israel's behalf.

Asked to reveal how he had obtained the classified information, he at first refused to answer. Finally he disclosed that Coptic friends who at one time had been high officials in the British mandatory government had supplied him with information and that other details had been picked up in conversation with Coptic Arabs.

His answers did not satisfy his interrogators. They were convinced that there was an espionage ring working with the priest. Al Antoni was detained on charges of spying, and the investigation continued.

Two Arab infiltrators sharing the same cell with the priest were about to be released, and Al Antoni asked them to get word to certain persons in Jordan that he had been arrested.

Ahmed Saalmah Abu Maarish, one of the infiltrators, was a professional smuggler who considered himself an Arab patriot, but according to his own personal standard, which was best summed up by his world view: there were those who could help Abu Maarish and there were those who could hinder him. In Al Antoni's case he decided it would be best to tell the Israeli authorities everything he had heard lest they suspect him of being involved with the Copt.

At first Al Antoni was cautious in talking to the two infiltrators. But when Abu Maarish mentioned that he was returning to Jordan upon his release and that he was acquainted with many officers of the Arab Legion, including Sadek Nazif, an officer of Circassian origin who represented Jordan on the mixed armistice commission, Al Antoni's face brightened. "Merciful Allah has sent you to me to help the holy Arab cause," he exclaimed. "When you get to the Old City, go to Nazif and deliver the following message: 'The Coptic priest is in prison. No one knows about his activities. They question him day and night but he is strong as a rock. He hasn't divulged anything.'"

Al Antoni also asked Abu Maarish to try to get the U.N. to pressure for his release.

"What have those sons of dogs got against you?" the infiltrator asked.

"Not a thing," the priest replied. "That Israeli customs inspector was an ass. I tricked him. Let them search the sewers of Jerusalem." He laughed, then added, "It's too bad I wrote out the name of Israel defense locations on the papers they did find. I should have used abbreviations."

Al Antoni also asked Abu Maarish to convey a message to the Coptic Church in Jordan: "Your priest has been arrested. Do not worry, he hasn't talked. As for the papers they found, he has claimed that they were for a book he is writing. They are still questioning him but he won't change his story. Make sure you confirm this. Warn the others."

Instead of delivering the priest's messages, Abu Maarish reported everything he had heard to the Israeli police.

Al Antoni's trial was held *in camera,* so it is impossible to determine the extent and true value of the intelligence he succeeded in obtaining. The papers and documents found among his belongings and Abu Maarish's testimony regarding his prison conversations with the accused were evidently conclusive evidence. Some details emerged from the closed trial to reveal that the Coptic leader was in contact with Egyptian intelligence in 1956, the time of serious infiltrations by Fedayeen units against Israeli border settlements. The Fedayeen incursions launched from Jordan and Lebanon were controlled by two Egyptian intelligence officers—in Jordan, Colonel Azzam Hilmi Al Mirzi, and in Lebanon, Captain Ali Halil. They arranged a meeting with Al Antoni during one of the priest's numerous trips to Arab Jerusalem. The Egyptian officers brought him regards and a letter from the head of the Coptic Church in Egypt. The letter asked the head of the church in Israel to "act in behalf of the sacred Arab cause." It did not specifically indicate spying, but apparently Al Antoni needed no further encouragement as he had frequent rendezvous with Al Mirzi and Halil.

At the trial he admitted meeting the Egyptian officers once during a visit to the Egyptian consul in the Old City. He maintained that he had merely conversed with the officers and persisted in his claim that he had never spied against Israel and was not an Egyptian agent. In his defense the priest said he was a loyal friend of Israel and had always enjoyed excellent relations with the government. In the later stages of the trial he tried to create the impression that he was some kind of double agent by seeking to cast suspicion on others. Details of his method of obtaining information through a network of informers in Israel and the use of his church in Jaffa as a cover for his activities were, however, conclusive evidence, and he was convicted and sentenced to twelve years imprisonment.

In his summing up, the Israel prosecutor charged Al Antoni with "profaning the holiness of the cloth," and added:

> This is one of the most serious cases of espionage uncovered in Israel. When one considers the evidence presented in court, it is clear that the defendant considered himself immune to discovery because of the official privileges he enjoyed. It is indeed difficult to ensure the safety of Israel when we have to contend with people like the accused who are trusted and treated in a special way by the state.

If Al Antoni had any idea that he would be treated as a martyr by his church, he was mistaken. In a letter to the state of Israel, Metropolitan Gabriel, the patriarch of the Coptic Church in the Middle East, stated that Al Antoni had been dismissed from his position and would no longer be permitted to conduct worship. The letter was seen as a clear indication that the Coptic Church, despite its Arab character, was neutral in the Arab-Israeli dispute and that any Copt who interpreted the church's stand otherwise would not be defended by the sect.

Al Antoni was released on November 20, 1964, after serving only seven years of his twelve-year sentence. He immediately left for Cairo where he lives today.

## ❧  "The Journalist"

On a Saturday evening in July, 1958, sixty-six convicted Arab infiltrators and spies broke out of Shattah prison in Israel's Jezreel Valley, three miles from the Jordanian border. Many of the prisoners serving long sentences at Shattah were captured Fedayeen terrorists. Eleven were killed in the Shattah break, including some guards and Jewish prisoners. The escapees fled to Jordan after breaking into the prison arsenal, killing the guard, and emptying it of submachine guns, rifles, and pistols.

The prison break became a major scandal in Israel, as public opinion, fueled by the press, expressed anger over the apparent incompetence and bungling of the penal authorities. Parliament appointed an inquiry committee, and the minister of police appointed his own departmental commission to investigate the lax security measures at Shattah. Editorials demanded to know how a maximum-security prison housing dangerous Arab terrorists and spies could be located only a few minutes from the Jordanian frontier and surrounded by fields and forests which offered good hiding places. The fact that the prison was near several large kibbutzim whose members could have been summoned had the alarm been given further emphasized the prison's inefficient system.

Subsequent investigations revealed that the escape had been planned in advance and had it not been for several

Jewish prisoners, the number of escaped Arabs would have been higher. As in any jail housing long-term prisoners, the old-timers knew the routine thoroughly—the guard shifts, location of the arsenal, and the best time to stage a break. Security was at its weakest at the end of the week when the warden and chief assistants went home for the Sabbath. Command of the prison on Saturday was assigned on a rotation basis to one officer, three sergeants, and skeleton crew of warders. Shattah was also the scene of a humanitarian experiment involving an attempt to rehabilitate certain prisoners by making them trustees responsible for tasks that in other prisons would be assigned to guards. Some of the trustees carried keys to the main gate and others were free to roam the prison grounds.

On the day of the break the prisoners had finished their work weaving reed mats in the workrooms near the outer gate and were returned to the inner courtyard prior to supper and the nightly lock-up.

Shortly after 6 P.M. a trustee named Subchi, an Egyptian student convicted of spying, approached a few of the prisoners in the inner courtyard. They asked the Egyptian to permit them to sweep the outer courtyard clean of the reed scraps that had accumulated there. Subchi agreed, and as soon as he opened the gate, about twenty prisoners, led by an Egyptian named Achmed Utman, ran through the courtyard carrying flaming torches made from bunches of reeds dipped in gasoline. They rushed to the guard room and disconnected the intercom and the alarm systems. From there they stormed the arsenal and, finding it locked, fanned out through the prison corridors searching for the sergeant on duty who had the key.

The guards stationed on the wall's watchtower did not sense what was happening within the jail. A Jewish prisoner spotted Utman in one of the hall corridors and knocked the Egyptian out with an iron bar, then locked him in a cell and alerted some of the guards who began firing at the escaping prisoners. Meanwhile a few of the prisoners had killed the sergeant in charge of the arsenal and stolen the key. Soon they were handing out submachine guns, rifles, and pistols to their fellow prisoners. The mutiny spread to the entire prison as convicts were handed weapons and shot the locks off the cell doors. Utman, who had regained consciousness, also shot the lock off the cell he was in and made his way to the outside gate of Shattah. There he directed the fleeing prisoners to run in small groups to the nearby Jordanian border.

The few armed guards on the grounds were insufficient to stem the flow of escaping prisoners, and the guards on the tower had not opened fire when they saw the mass of convicts streaming out of the compound into the total darkness of the outer grounds. One of the guards later said that he was afraid of committing mass murder.

The cycle of bungling was complete. By the time guards had organized themselves to resist the break, 66 of the 190 prisoners were gone.

On the basis of intensive interrogation and investigation of the circumstances of the break, the inquiry commission concluded that the Shattah mutiny was the work of Egyptian intelligence. Four Egyptian students serving ten-year terms for espionage had led the first stage of the outbreak. Another Egyptian, Achmed Batet, a newcomer to Shattah, had then taken over the escape from the students. The brains behind the prison break was Utman, who was known by the nickname, "the Journalist."

Utman, who had been sent to Shattah on suspicion of espionage six weeks before the escape, had quickly become the leader of the Arab prisoners at the prison. They paid tribute to him by bringing him smuggled cigarettes, fruit, and other delicacies, all of which he accepted as his due. The force of his personality, his wit, erudition, and bearing enabled him to win the confidence of the convicted spies and terrorists surrounding him. Together with a few trusted fellow Egyptian prisoners, he had studied Shattah's routine and structure and spotted its weak points in less than two months.

Here was surely one of the most impressive Egyptian operatives ever captured by Israeli counterespionage. His unusual method of entering the country—unusual for a spy— and his brazen self-confidence and high degree of intelligence marked him as a unique agent.

Utman came from a wealthy, aristocratic Cairene family. After completing his studies, he joined the Egyptian foreign service. His first post was cultural attaché in Jidda, Saudi Arabia. After returning to Cairo, he was made head of the foreign news section of the Ministry of Information and Popular Enlightenment. He was known to every foreign correspondent in the Egyptian capital as pleasant, intelligent, and exceedingly shrewd. His job consisted of censoring correspondents' dispatches and deleting any unfavorable references to Egypt contained in their reports. He would favor journalists who wrote positive things about the country and Nasser by giving them interviews with ranking Egyptian military commanders. Occasionally he would seek to recruit a correspondent as a spy or propagandist.

In 1956, Utman was sent to Paris and, because of the tension between Egypt and France at that time, was immediately placed under surveillance by the Deuxieme Bureau, the French internal security agency.

For several weeks he made no move. He hung around cafés and strolled through the city. Then Utman approached the leaders of an anti-Nasser Egyptian émigré group who had set up a broadcasting service in France. He offered them his services, passing himself off as a refugee who had left Egypt after becoming disillusioned with Nasser's regime. As the son of a large landowner whose estates had been confiscated by the government, Utman's story seemed convincing. He then penetrated Egyptian émigré circles in France and made contact with the leaders of the anti-Nasser opposition who were subsidized by the French government in the hope that one day Nasser would be overthrown and the new regime drawn from the present exiled opposition would be friendly to France.

Utman reported the names of the opposition leaders to Egyptian intelligence which in turn arrested their relatives in an attempt to use them as hostages. In this way Nasser hoped to silence his opponents abroad and force them to return to Egypt to stand trial.

Another one of Utman's assignments, and the one that was to expose him, was to obtain information on French-Israeli relations. High priority was placed on this task, because at that time Israel, France, and Britain were planning the Suez Campaign and Egyptian intelligence had gotten wind of something. But as soon as Utman made a move in this direction, French counterespionage seized him and had him deported to Egypt.

Little is known about what Utman did upon his return to Cairo. He was known to have been in close contact with Egyptian intelligence and met several times with Ali Sabry, Nasser's deputy and right-hand man in charge of espionage. These details of Utman's activities in Paris and Cairo were found out later after investigation by Israeli intelligence. But in September, 1957, when Utman showed up at the Israel embassy in London and asked to speak to the official in charge of political activities, nothing was known about him. No details of Utman's career in Paris had been furnished by the French to Israeli intelligence.

He introduced himself as an anti-Nasser newspaperman prepared to work in Israel. He suggested broadcasting anti-Nasser propaganda from Jerusalem in an effort to incite antiregime sentiment among the Egyptian people.

The embassy people were naturally suspicious of but also impressed with Utman. His request was forwarded to the appropriate agency in Israel, and two weeks later "the Journalist" landed at Tel Aviv's Lydda Airport. The tall, slightly balding, athletic Egyptian registered at Tel Aviv's expensive Dan Hotel. He was kept under surveillance and allowed to move about freely. He visited bars, went to the theater, and spent time sight-seeing. He was not detected doing anything unusual. In fact, he acted rather like a listless tourist.

Israeli officials met with him, and in their conversations Utman displayed a thorough acquaintance with Nasser and his aides. His comments indicated that he was up on Egyptian politics and other matters such as land reform and economic problems. In addition to Arabic, he spoke English, French, and German fluently. Even his Hebrew was rather good. Suspicion grew when he began speaking Russian and Polish. Ordinarily Egyptians do not visit the Soviet-bloc countries, and it was fairly obvious that he had been sent there by the government and had stayed long enough to learn the languages. Still this was only circumstantial evidence, and Israeli intelligence had no proof that "the Journalist" was a spy.

Utman continued to stay at the Dan Hotel and voice anti-Nasser sentiments in conversation with Israeli intelligence officers. At the same time Israel's security services sought to piece together a picture of his earlier career in Egypt, London, and Paris.

After a month the Israelis began asking him when he intended to start his propaganda broadcasts. After stalling for a few days, Utman finally presented Israeli intelligence with a daring plan to jeopardize Nasser's rule. He proposed to return to Cairo and recruit several of his anti-Nasser friends for a sabotage ring that would carry out terrorist attacks within Egyptian territory.

"If you wish to topple Nasser," he passionately told the Israelis, "prove to his opponents that they have a chance of success. Strike at the center of power. Make life a terror for the members of the military clique so that they'll be forced to stay in relative seclusion. When people see that Nasser himself is afraid to make public appearances, his opponents will rise up and finish him off."

Utman spoke with authority and conviction. "What would prevent us from setting off a time bomb in a car next to the Ministry of Defense. Just imagine a bomb exploding while a meeting of Nasser's Revolutionary Council was taking place—boom!—no more Nasser, no more Marshall Amer."

He also suggested sabotage attempts against foreign embassies in Cairo in order to implicate Nasser and worsen relations between his regime and foreign governments.

When asked how he would obtain explosives and other equipment and find accomplices for these plots, he shrugged and calmly replied, "Such small details are unimportant. Besides your agents [Israeli agents in Cairo] can probably help us."

Utman's incredible proposal further strengthened suspicion, but there was still not enough evidence against him to warrant an arrest. No one was willing to pass final judgment without concrete evidence. Then a few days later an Egyptian-Jewish couple who had fled from persecution in Egypt spotted Utman as they passed by his hotel. They immediately reported to the police that he had been their neighbor in Cairo and was known as a member of Egyptian intelligence. They said that more than once they had considered appealing to him when they were subject to threats and harassment by the Egyptian police.

On the basis of the couple's identification, Utman was arrested as an enemy agent that same day, in November of 1957, and held pending investigation. He denied that he had been sent to Israel by Egyptian intelligence in order to involve Israel in embarrassing international incidents and to uncover Israeli agents in Egypt.

Following his arrest, Egypt's newspapers came out with banner headlines announcing that an Egyptian had been kidnapped by Israel in cooperation with France. The papers claimed that Utman had been tortured to extract a confession.

While awaiting the conclusion of the investigation against him, Utman carried out the Shattah prison break. But he himself was wounded in the legs and unable to escape.

At his trial he steadfastly refused to admit that he was an Egyptian agent. For his part in the Shattah escape he was sentenced in June, 1960 to six years imprisonment and was released in April, 1966. He is now believed to be in Cairo.

During his years of imprisonment Utman continually submitted imaginative briefs appealing his conviction. He also took great pride in the part he had played in engineering the Shattah escape and toward the end of his prison term no longer concealed his connection with Egyptian intelligence. He freely gave interviews to Israeli reporters. Asked once how it was that his Hebrew was so good, he replied that every Egyptian intelligence officer is required to study Hebrew, "but of course I improved it here."

One positive result of Israel's encounter with Achmed Utman is that not one prisoner has escaped from Shattah prison since that summer night in 1958. "The Journalist" had taught his captors a lesson.

# ❧  "The Lone Wolf"

ON A DAMP EVENING IN DECEMBER, 1963, IN A POOR section of Ashkelon on Israel's Mediterranean coast bordering the Gaza Strip, a police vehicle stopped in front of a small cement house. Four uniformed policemen surrounded the house and two plain-clothes detectives knocked on the door, which bore the nameplate "Yitzhak Kochuk." They entered without waiting for an answer and arrested the sole occupant of the dwelling. One of the officers took out a pair of handcuffs and read the arrest warrant: "Kobruk Yaakovian, alias Yitzhak Ben Solomon 'Jacky' Kochuk, you are hereby accused of spying against the state of Israel for Egyptian intelligence."

Yaakovian was too shocked to resist. After his removal to the Ashkelon police station, the simple immigrant's hut was searched thoroughly. A well-equipped darkroom, electronic communications equipment, and bottles of disappearing ink were found on the premises. Israel's security forces derived special satisfaction from the arrest of Yaakovian, an Armenian from Cairo who had been planted in Israel after long and careful preparations by Egypt's espionage services.

Kobruk's connection with Egypt's intelligence apparatus had begun a few years earlier in Cairo where, as a multilingual photographer, the young Armenian was arrested by the police on suspicion of some minor transgression, then

116

convicted and sentenced to two and a half months in prison. While serving his time, he was visited on several occasions by an Egyptian intelligence officer who finally invited him to join the service. After his release he signed a three-year contract with the government security service.

For some time Egypt's military command had been unhappy with the results of the various intelligence-gathering agencies, especially insofar as Israel was concerned. Twice daily, reports were forwarded to Ali Sabry, Nasser's minister for presidential affairs and the man in charge of coordinating political and military matters for the Egyptian ruler. The special files consisted of translations of Hebrew newspaper reports and summaries of dispatches from Egyptian agents in the field. Whatever pertained to Israel received special attention at Sabry's meetings with Nasser. As one of the most intelligent members of the military clique, Ali Sabry was perceptive and even tempered, in contrast to most of his colleagues. He tried to develop a realistic appraisal of Israel's military strength without being blinded by the emotional and patriotic compulsions of his comrades. Amid the reams of reports from Egyptian diplomats, foreign press summaries, and other sources of information, it was often difficult to discern what information was useful and relevant. Occasionally Sabry would try to guide the leaders of Egyptian intelligence. He would point to the stacks of reports on Israel and say something to the effect of, "Very interesting but that's not it." He would thumb through the summaries based on the information conveyed by infiltrators and agents which told of Israeli army troop movements, installations, and other details and sadly say, "This isn't it. This doesn't give us the picture."

The intelligence officers would explain the low level of espionage by pointing out that Palestinian refugee infiltrators and Fedayeen commandos could not be relied upon for accurate estimates of military strength. They could not penetrate Israeli camps. Sabry told them that without such information they were groping in thin air. "If we don't know exactly how many new tanks there are in Israel's armored corps and the weapon strength of other units, our military intelligence amounts to nothing more than gossip." He would add, "We must reach the stage where we receive a steady flow of information on what's happening inside Israel's armed forces, even if it takes years to accomplish this."

But no improvement was noted. The quality of incoming intelligence remained inferior, and Egyptian agents continued to be caught in Israel by the score. Even replacing the heads of Egyptian Central Intelligence was of no avail.

In 1959, Nasser's regime turned to several former Nazi intelligence officers for advice. The Germans, most of them war criminals, had found a safe refuge in Egypt. Their advice was to concentrate in the future on the penetration of Israel by espionage agents who would work independently of any existing ring and would, under well-constructed covers, reside in Israel for long periods of time without being pressured for immediate results. Kobruk Yaakovian was trained to be this type of operative.

In December, 1961, Yaakovian, traveling under the name Yitzhak Ben Solomon Kochuk, sat in one of the lounges of the passenger liner SS *Pota* and watched the excited European, North African, and South American Jews milling about him. The boat was approaching Haifa, and the officials of the Jewish Agency, the Israeli quasi-governmental organization responsible for immigration and absorption, had set up tables in the lounge to begin processing the new immigrants. Patiently Yaakovian waited his turn. He placed his documents on the table—an immigrant visa, No. 180598, issued by the Israeli embassy in Río de Janeiro and a refugee certificate issued by the United Nations to a Jew

of Turkish ancestry who had emigrated from Egypt and had
lived in Brazil before leaving for Israel.

The Jewish Agency official perused the documents and the
questionnaires Yaakovian had filled out.

"Occupation?"

"Photographer," Kobruk replied.

"Any relatives in Israel?"

"No. But I have some friends at Kibbutz Bror Chail in the
Negev. The Argaman family; they expect me. I'd like to go
there."

The Agency man made a notation: "Sent to Kibbutz Bror
Chail." A second official supplied the new immigrant with
bus tickets, and a third gave Kobruk a document stating that
as a new immigrant he was entitled to receive government
housing. He was also given directions on how to reach the
kibbutz by bus from Haifa. By this short procedure Yaakovian entered Israel while posing as a new immigrant. There
was nothing in his manner or Semitic appearance to dis-
tinguish him from hundreds of thousands of oriental Jews
who had preceded him to the homeland.

At the kibbutz he was greeted warmly by Eli and Bracha
Argaman, who called him Jacky. That evening Yaakovian
sat with Argamans after supper and reminisced about their
meeting on a ship bound for Brazil six months earlier. It was
during that voyage that the Armenian had become friendly
with the young Israeli couple who were on their way to visit
Eli's parents in Río de Janeiro. The Argamans and their
young children had boarded the ship in Haifa, and Kobruk
came aboard when it stopped at Genoa.

The Armenian was immediately successful with the
Argaman children. He took their pictures, told them stories,
and treated them to ice cream and candy at every port. His
politeness and cheerful manner also helped him win over
the parents. They were sympathetic when they heard his

story. He recounted that he had been born in Turkey and had emigrated with his parents to Egypt. There he had been orphaned and left alone in the world. He showed the Israeli couple a picture of what he said was his mother's grave in Cairo's Jewish cemetery. He gave the impression of a Jew who felt strongly about his people's destiny, and he displayed an earnest curiosity about Israel. He even tried to improve his limited Hebrew during the voyage by practicing with the Argamans.

In Río de Janeiro, Eli introduced his new friend Jacky to his parents, and the Egyptian came to know the elder Argamans well. When Eli and his family returned to Israel after a two-month stay, Jacky was at the boat to see them off. They exchanged the Hebrew greeting, "Lehitraot," meaning "see you again," and Eli told Jacky that since he was about to begin a new life he should think of settling in Israel. Jacky smiled and replied, "Who knows? Everything's possible."

During the return voyage to Israel, Eli and his wife often spoke of Jacky and his curious ignorance of Jewish history and customs. Though the Armenian had often mentioned his attendance at the Cairo synagogue, he didn't know what a prayer shawl was. Recalling his conversations with Jacky, Eli later told his wife, "I wanted to tell him something about Zionism, but he was so ignorant that I had to start with Abraham the Patriarch." As a native-born Israeli, Eli perhaps took it for granted that every Jew knew certain basic things. His wife tried to convince him that this was not always the case with Diaspora Jews, but Eli still had a funny feeling about Jacky's Jewish "background."

After a week at the Argaman's kibbutz, Jacky decided to enroll in Ulpan—a government-sponsored Hebrew course for new immigrants. The Jewish Agency placed him at an Ulpan at Kibbutz Negba near the Gaza Strip. There he joined a group of fifty other newcomers, but Yaakovian was an indifferent student. His teacher thought that perhaps this was because he knew more Hebrew than his classmates at the outset. He kept to himself and spent many hours in his room, listening to music and foreign news broadcasts, especially those from Arab countries. There was nothing unusual in this since many immigrants from Moslem countries regularly listened to Arab radio stations. Jacky stayed at Negba six months and did not attract undue attention.

He spent time wandering around the settlement and the surrounding area and with his sophisticated camera taking pictures of landscapes, deserted trenches, and pillboxes, remnants of Negba's stand against the Egyptian army during the War of Liberation in 1948. He developed his own pictures, and few members of the kibbutz recall ever seeing them.

Despite his withdrawal from the settlement's life he became friendly with Mira, one of the kibbutz girls. She was barely sixteen and Jacky was twenty-eight, but their friendship quickly developed into romance. Mira, who had grown up in the idyllic, sheltered kibbutz atmosphere, was entranced by Jacky's stories of other countries and his travels. The kibbutz members were unhappy over the relationship. They felt that Jacky was not of their kind and they could not accept him. They sought to protect Mira and tried to persuade her to end the affair.

Nevertheless, the men and women of Negba felt a certain sympathy toward the new immigrant. He would tell them how his father had deserted his mother and how devoted his mother had been to him despite their hardships. Like other Jews of a Levantine background, Jacky had great facility with language. He spoke Arabic, Turkish, French, German, Italian, Spanish, and Hebrew. His intelligence seemed quick rather than profound, but this was characteristically oriental in that he was incapable of being analytical. When asked where he had learned so many languages, he replied that he had picked them up as a child while wandering with his mother in search of his father.

He was very moody and some days would just lie in his bed staring at the ceiling. When the kibbutz secretary approached him about leaving Mira and allowing her to continue her studies, he gave a resolute answer: "I love her and intend to marry her."

At the conclusion of the course he applied to the Jewish Agency for housing in Ashkelon. In accordance with his request they assigned him a small house in South Ashkelon, a typical new immigrants' quarter populated mostly by North African Jews. Agency officials could not understand why as a single man he wanted to settle in a remote part of Ashkelon, away from the center, when it would seem more natural for him to settle near Tel Aviv or one of the other larger cities. Bue the cement house near the Gaza Strip suited Kobruk Yaakovian perfectly.

Shortly after settling in Ashkelon, he was called to military service. He tried to join the armored corps but was assigned to a transportation unit. He was unhappy in the army and often told Eli Argaman during his visits to Bror Chail that his duties were beneath his dignity. Eli helped Jacky apply for an early release from the service on the grounds that at twenty-eight he was out of place in an army in which most of the soldiers were eighteen- and nineteen-year-olds. Another reason for his application was that he intended to marry. To Eli's surprise, the request was granted and Jacky moved back to his house in Ashkelon.

He made some desultory attempts at getting a job as a commercial or press photographer. Occasionally he would go to Tel Aviv to answer an advertisement but always reported failure on his return. He complained bitterly that he was being discriminated against and began spending his days in Ashkelon's cafés, sitting with new immigrants and soldiers on leave. In discussions he would defend Nasser, arguing that while the Egyptian ruler might be bad for Israel and minority groups in Egypt, he was the best ruler that country had ever had. Although he was invited to his neighbors' homes, Jacky's only two visitors during the two years he lived in Ashkelon were Mira and a young friend named Albert Amiel who would stay with him whenever he visited Ashkelon.

Jacky's idle life, café conversations and his frequent mentions of a forthcoming trip to Italy, where he said he had a sum of money on deposit, eventually brought him to the attention of Israeli security officers. For a short time he worked as a truck driver for a firm that was drilling oil wells in the vicinity of Ashkelon. People were puzzled and wondered how he managed to live without working most of the time.

He confided to Mira that he was unhappy in Israel and said that since he could not find work in his field, he would be better off going away.

Counterintelligence began a regular surveillance of his daily routine and noted that he frequently received registered mail from Europe. Examinations of the letters in a lab revealed that between the innocuous lines of writing, detailed instructions on what military information Jacky was to seek and report back had been written in invisible ink, which when treated with a solution became legible. He would send back the information written in invisible ink to several addresses in Europe. When counterespionage was satisfied that its investigation was complete, it moved in on Yaakovian.

It was subsequently revealed that he was the first Egyptian agent to be caught who had been planted as a "lone wolf" operative. Egyptian intelligence had invested years of planning and preparation in Yaakovian. His mission represented a decisive shift in Egyptian espionage thinking, for until the Armenian's arrest the Arab states had not been

known to engage in this type of long-range spying. Yaakovian's case revealed a fairly thorough picture of Egypt's
espionage apparatus. Significantly, it showed that Nasser
regarded Israel as a long-term threat and was willing to
adapt his strategy to this view.

As a young Armenian, Yaakovian resembled many young
Jews from the oriental communities. During the whole of
1960 he was trained in cryptography, microfilming, espionage photography, and communications. Then he was
taught about Israel's political system, society, and geogra-
phy. He also studied Hebrew. To construct his cover as a
Jewish emigrant from Turkey named Yitzhak Ben Solomon
Kochuk, he began visiting the Cairo synagogue and even
underwent circumcision.

Egyptian intelligence gave him an identification card,
and with it he applied to the United Nations in Cairo for a
refugee certificate on the grounds that the Egyptian authorities refused to extend his stay in that country. He then
applied to the Brazilian consulate and received an immigrant's visa. This type of approach was feasible because
of Israel's open immigration policy extending to all Jews.

On his way to Brazil he continued to develop his cover
and became friendly with the Argamans for that purpose. In
Río de Janeiro he visited synagogues and joined Jewish
youth groups. In the Brazilian capital his contact was Salem
Aziz Es Said, the chief of Egyptian intelligence agents in
Brazil, who posed as the head of an Egyptian trading
Agency.

With Es Said's help Yaakovian received a Brazilian identification card as a Jew. He worked as a photographer and
made many Jewish acquaintances. After approximately a
year in Brazil he approached the Jewish Agency in Río de
Janeiro and expressed a desire to settle in Israel.

His transportation to Italy was arranged by the Agency
and he was given a ticket for the immigrant ship SS *Pota,*

as any other Jew from South America might have been. Yaakovian's final instructions from Es Said were to behave just like any other new immigrant. "Live a normal life, try to join an armored unit, and after fully acclimating yourself to the country, commence your espionage work."

The Armenian's arrest came as a shock to Kibbutz Negba, those who had served with him in the army, and his neighbors in Ashkelon. The Argamans were less surprised than most, as they had always felt there was something queer about their friend Jacky.

With the episode of Kobruk Yaakovian a new stage of escalation in the "war of intellects" between the intelligence services of Israel and her Arab enemies was revealed. It was clear that Egypt was no longer content to rely on infiltrators and short-range incursions over the border or on the recruitment of local Arabs who would clandestinely travel back and forth from Israel to the Gaza Strip.

Kobruk Yaakovian was indicted on nine counts of espionage. He confessed to eight of the charges and was sentenced to eighteen years imprisonment.

PART III

# ❦ Phase II of "The Final Solution"
# The Germans in Nasser's Service

A**T THE END OF THE SECOND WORLD WAR REPORTS** circulated in Europe that several hundred Germans, deserters from the Afrika Korps, had obtained asylum in Egypt. Egypt's readiness to provide a refuge for Nazis came as no surprise. During the war there had been considerable pro-German sentiment in the country, which was under British control. The sympathy shown to the Axis was seen as an Egyptian reaction to British colonialism. The deserters were soon joined by many war criminals fleeing from Allied war crimes trials. Farouk welcomed the SS officers, concentration camp officials, and other key figures in the Nazi plan to annihilate European Jewry, known euphemistically as "the final solution of the Jewish problem." In Europe an underground led by former SS men and aided by survivors among Nazi officers operated an effective underground railway that spirited wanted Nazis out of Europe to South America and the Arab lands of the Middle East. Forged passports and hiding places in Catholic monasteries in Rome facilitated the escape to Egypt.

Egypt's first major utilization of Nazi experts was in 1950 when King Farouk had a group of German economists and industrial managers under the direction of Wilhelm Foss, the former director of the Skoda munitions works who had arrived in Egypt at Farouk's invitation in 1948, lay the foundation for the Egyptian munitions industry. They found that their task was made impossible by the lack of trained Egyptian personnel. Foss had also been helpful in the reorganization of the Egyptian army following its defeat in 1948 by Israel. At his behest a group of ranking Nazi army officers was brought to Egypt and set about revamping that country's armed forces. At the head of this Nazi military assistance mission was the former Wehrmacht infantry commander, General Wilhelm Pfermbecher.

Until the Soviet Union became Egypt's principal military supplier in the late 1950's, the Germans in Cairo enjoyed a privileged status. Because they were careful to avoid involvement in domestic politics, their position did not suffer at the time of the "Free Officers" revolt in 1954. Under the new regime, in fact, the Nazi advisers were held in even higher esteem, as their anti-Jewish records guaranteed their usefulness and loyalty to the anti-Israeli orientation of Nasser's government.

Egypt's experience in the Sinai Campaign of 1956, however, led to the diminished influence of the German military advisers, who were made to serve as scapegoats for the humiliating defeat by Israel. With the introduction of Soviet and Czechoslovak military instructors in 1957, most of the German military advisers were relegated to second-rate positions. By this time the number of Nazi refugees in Egypt had reached several thousand. One of the best-known former Nazis was Professor Jonathan Von Leers who had been one of Goebbels' chief assistants and was wanted as a war criminal. Shortly after World War II he escaped with his family to Argentina, but with the overthrow of dictator Juan Perón in 1955, Von Leers, like many other Germans in Argentina, feared that the new regime would be less zealous in protecting Nazi criminals from Israeli agents already hunting for Adolf Eichmann, Martin Bormann, and Dr. Mangele, the sadistic "Angel of Death" of Auschwitz. Von Leers was able to obtain a proper passport from the

West German embassy in Buenos Aires and left for Egypt where he was immediately employed as an army instructor in the art of anti-Semitic propaganda.

Von Leers was only one of many prominent Nazi criminals enjoying protected status in Nasser's Egypt. From time to time Israel would bring this fact to Bonn's attention, but the West German government claimed that it was powerless to bring these men to justice. This reaction was not unexpected, for there were so many former Nazis living unharmed in West Germany—some holding government posts—that the existence of Nazis in Egypt was hardly likely to arouse concern.

Egyptian-Soviet friendship was at its height in 1957 and 1958; the Russians were sending large quantities of armaments to Nasser and had promised to help finance the Aswan Dam. The friendship cooled, however, when the Soviet Union informed Nasser that it could not meet his requests for spare parts for the MIG-15. At first the Soviets said they had stopped manufacturing these parts and were now constructing MIG-19 and 21 aircraft—models that were still top secret. Nasser realized how dependent he was on Russia. The MIG-15's were useless to his air force without spare parts. He appealed to Khrushchev and was told that the necessary parts would be supplied on condition that they were paid for in hard currency rather than with cotton. The Egyptian leader balked at this arrangement because he felt the Russians were asking too high a price.

Nasser notified his military attachés in the capitals of Europe and asked them to ascertain the availability of European, particularly German, scientists and technicians to establish munitions factories in Egypt. Within a short time he had indications that hundreds, perhaps thousands of Germans would be glad to move to Egypt and work for his war machine.

At the suggestion of Colonel Ramadan, the Egyptian

military attaché in Berne, Nasser invited to Cairo the famous Nazi aircraft designer Willi Messerschmidt, who at
that time was busy at the Hispano-Switza works in Spain
manufacturing several new planes of his own design.
Messerschmidt was accorded a regal welcome in Cairo and
after a few meetings with Nasser agreed to undertake the
construction of aircraft plants in Egypt. Air Marshal Sidky
Pasha, a commander of the Egyptian air force, was im-
mensely pleased with the arrangement and, with typical
Levantine exaggeration, predicted an air force equipped
with hundreds of new fighter planes, all made in Egypt.
The first contract called for the manufacture of a supersonic jet fighter that was superior to anything Israel had.

Messerschmidt chose Professor Ferdinand Brandtner, a
German of Austrian origin who was chief designer of the
Junkers works under the Nazis, as manager of the Egyptian
plant. Brandtner had already been in Egypt for some time,
and his Nazi record recommended him to Nasser's government. At the end of the Second World War, Brandtner,
along with eight hundred aeronautical engineers, had been
arrested and imprisoned in the Soviet Union. But Brandtner
concluded that his skill as a scientist would be of interest
to his captors and he sought an interview with officials of
Russian military research. He told them that he was aware
of their difficulties with turbine propellers and said he could
easily assist them in overcoming the obstacles keeping their
research some five years behind the West. The Kremlin
agreed and soon Brandtner was once again directing the
eight hundred German technicians he had been captured
with. In 1957 he succeeded in producing the first turbo
propeller of its kind, and it was used in Russia's Tupolev-114
plane. Brandtner was released and returned to West
Germany where he encountered difficulties in finding employment. Even in West Germany the professor who had
faithfully served the Nazis and then switched to the

Russians seemed a bit too flexible to trust. He moved on to Egypt and gained Nasser's confidence by his optimistic plans to convert Egypt to the leading producer of fighter planes for the Afro-Asian bloc.

Once the Messerschmidt contract was signed, Brandtner returned to Europe to purchase materials and machinery. He visited the Heinkel Messerschmidt and Mercedes Benz companies and recruited many of his former colleagues and subordinates with tempting salary offers. Part of the appeal of his offer was the chance to develop an Egyptian air force that would play a key role in the destruction of Israel. It was an irresistible combination: the name Messerschmidt, huge sums of money, and an ideological motive congruent with the Nazi sympathies of these German men of science.

Work was conducted under elaborate security arrangements. In Hiluan, a suburb of Cairo, two separate factories were built. In one the Messerschmidt bodies were constructed. In the second Brandtner personally supervised engine assembly.

Although the project operated under strictest secrecy, Israeli intelligence was able to find out enough to doubt that the planes would ever be produced in sufficient numbers to constitute a threat to Israel. The serious problems of organization and construction emanating from the low technical level of the Egyptian employees made it unlikely that the program would ever be a success. Messerschmidt had predicted that mass production of two supersonic models—the HA-200 and HA-300—would begin by 1965. These models had already been produced at the Messerschmidt plant in Spain and utilized a British Bristol–Siddeley Orpheus jet engine. Despite a huge investment of manpower and an expenditure of more than $450 million, production dragged far behind schedule. Finally a few modern Messerschmidts were produced with imported

parts—the first model was a two-seat trainer and the second
a one-seat supersonic fighter plane. Israel's military leaders
regarded the production of these few planes as having value
only as a means of bolstering the ego and prestige of the
Egyptian ruler.

The elaborate project and its meager results set off a
bitter internal debate among the members of Egypt's ruling
clique. The generals did not hide their disappointment. For
years they had hoped for an air force that would not be
dependent on the Soviet Union. One faction of the National
Defense Council advocated the discontinuance of the project, but this group was opposed by military leaders who felt
that the program should carry on. Nasser was absorbed in
the problem of achieving military superiority over Israel
and was convinced that, despite Egypt's immense ground
force and considerable Soviet-supplied air force, the country still could not risk an armed confrontation with the
Jewish state and be assured of its outcome. He once
summed up his thinking before the Defense Council in the
following manner:

> Ours is not a problem of quantity. We have hundreds
> of tanks and fighter planes. We have, thanks to Allah,
> numerical superiority in every type of armament but we
> don't dare risk a war with Israel. The next war must be
> short and decisive, because the U.N. and the world
> powers will not tolerate a prolonged war in the area.
> Accordingly, we have to be able to deal Israel one crip-
> pling blow.

Egypt's military leaders then adopted a new strategy,
the essence of which was that Israel was to be destroyed
not in a face-to-face confrontation but rather by remote-
controlled, unmanned rockets. Israel was small and the
bulk of her population centered in a fairly small area. Her
essential industries, located in a few cities, could easily be

destroyed in one day by ballistic missiles and she would be rendered incapable of retaliatory action.

With this plan in mind, Nasser turned to his German scientists and launched with their assistance a rocket-manufacturing program. This was in 1959. Three years of research and experimentation passed, and on "Revolution Day" in July, 1962, foreign military attachés stationed in Cairo were astounded when during the military parade celebrating the eighth anniversary of Nasser's regime two medium-range surface-to-surface missiles of Egyptian manufacture named the "Cairo" and the "Victory" were unveiled. Each rocket had a range of 350 miles, enough striking distance to reach any population center in Israel.

Despite the extraordinary security arrangements attending the rocket program, Israeli agents had kept abreast of developments since 1959.

In Israel first reports of Egypt's intensified rocket activity had been met with skepticism. Israeli military and government leaders privy to the intelligence assessments found it hard to believe that Egypt, her economy already strained in every sector and her cotton crop mortgaged for years to come to pay for arms purchases, would embark on a disastrously expensive stepped-up rocket venture after having spent millions of dollars on an unsuccessful aircraft construction program.

But further reports put an end to disbelief. This intelligence indicated that hundreds of additional German specialists had secretly arrived in Egypt in 1960 and 1961. Some plants were operating on three shifts daily, and consultant firms in Germany, Spain, and Switzerland were under contract to Nasser. The terrible picture that emerged revealed an Egyptian plan eventually to attack Israel with rockets aimed at strategic locations. This first attack, which would paralyze Israel at one blow, would then be followed up with artillery, armored, and air attacks to assure total destruction of the Jewish state. It was also discovered that one group of German scientists was working with poisonous gases and there was talk of chemical warfare as well as a scheme to poison the Sea of Galilee and other of Israel's sources of water.

Jerusalem was stunned by the scope and dimension of Nasser's diabolical plan. Bonn was officially notified of the activities of West German nationals in Egypt, and Israel constantly emphasized the horrible significance of German scientists working with Nasser to complete the aim of the Third Reich's "final solution." Israel's approaches were met with evasion on the part of the West German government, which claimed that it was powerless to act since the federal constitution guaranteed the right of German citizens to work wherever they wished.

There was no end to German judicial casuistry despite the direct challenge voiced by Israel's representatives: Didn't the Bonn government appreciate the significance of former followers of Hitler preparing another attempt to annihilate the Jewish people? Did post-war Germany forget that for the Jewish people Nasser was the self-acknowledged heir to Hitler's insane policies?

Appeals to Washington, London, and Paris also met with indifference, and Israel had no choice but to act offensively. The nation's security and espionage agencies were instructed to learn the identities of the Germans running the Egyptian rocket project, to determine exactly the program's progress, and to uncover the foreign suppliers servicing Nasser.

A list of scientists' names involved in the program was compiled after careful investigation. Professors Eugen Sanger, Paul Görcke, and Wolfgang Pilz were the overall directors of the secret Egyptian research and manufacturing programs. In addition, Dr. Heinz Krug and Dr. Hans Kleinwächter figured prominently in the Cairo operation.

Further investigation showed that these men were known rocket experts during the days of Hitler and had faithfully served the Nazis. Several of them had distinguished themselves in the field of experimentation with electronically guided missiles, and it was assumed that in this area Egypt had already passed the laboratory stage and gone on to the main problem of refining this capability so that rockets could be guided to specific projects in Israel.

As head of the Stuttgart Institute of Jet Propulsion, Professor Sanger was limited to research and not actual production because of the Four-Power agreement restricting German military activity. The institute was financed by public funds, but only a few members of the German government knew that Sanger was furnishing the Egyptian rocket industry with the results of his research in Stuttgart. Sanger's assistants at the Stuttgart institute were Görcke and Pilz. The latter had directed the wartime team responsible for the V-1 rocket that had terrorized London near the end of World War II. He had also worked for the French in the post-war period helping to develop the "Veronique" rocket. Pilz often claimed that he was a man of science, oblivious to the political implications of his work

Görcke had taught physics at several German universities and was noted for his work with radar and infrared rays. In 1952 he went to Egypt with the "Serva" group—a team of German experts who made a tentative beginning under King Farouk to develop a rocket center. This early German group was under the leadership of Professor Ralph Engel, subsequently the director of the Italian rocket industry. Görcke stayed on in Egypt and made many important contributions to Nasser's war effort in the areas of radar and electronics before returning to Germany to join Sanger at the Stuttgart institute. Sanger and his colleagues would regularly fly to Cairo to oversee operations and check on the progress of the various research projects.

When the German press reported that these men were in actuality running Nasser's rocket program, official circles in Bonn reacted angrily and accused Israel of leaking the news to inflate the significance of the issue. They maintained that the German scientists in Cairo were engaged in legitimate scientific activity and said it was preferable to have German scientists there rather than Russians who would gladly replace them.

The publicity given to the German scientists did nothing to move the government to action, but public opinion was sufficiently aroused to bring about Sanger's resignation from the institute. Pilz and Görcke left for Cairo, leaving behind Heinz Krug, an important member of the institute staff, to set up the "Intra" company in Stuttgart for the purpose of purchasing parts for the Cairo rocket program. Pilz and Görcke each had an interest in Intra and made fortunes on the commissions the company received for its transactions in Spain, Germany, and Switzerland. Krug later moved his operation to Munich where he was close to the office of Egyptian Airlines—a convenient arrangement for dispatching supplies to Cairo. He was also an active recruiter of engineers, physicists, and electronics experts for the Cairo rocket base.

At the same time, a secret recruitment office for foreign experts was set up in Switzerland under the direction of Colonel Ramadan, the Egyptian military attaché in Berne. He also maintained liaison with the MECO Corporation and the Motoren Turbinen Pumpen Company in Zurich. These firms were controlled by Kamil Hassan Said, a Swiss engineer of Egyptian origin, and they supplied the Cairo rocket program with parts, engines, and assembled bodies. They also negotiated contracts for Egypt and were successful in enlisting 250 German scientists for service in Egypt.

Toward the end of 1961, Israel learned that Nasser was

trying to obtain quantities of cobalt 60, a radioactive substance difficult to acquire in large amounts. The Egyptians had dispatched purchasing agents to Germany, Canada, and even India to acquire the chemical which, once obtained, was sent in parcels to Dr. Isis Halil, sister of Mahmud El-Din, the director of Egyptian rocket operations. The cobalt was then forwarded to the research section headed by Wolfgang Pilz. Israel was certain that Egypt was planning to manufacture rockets with nuclear striking heads and, despairing of any action on Bonn's part, decided to warn the German scientists in Nasser's employ of the terrible responsibility they had undertaken.

In September, 1962, Heinz Krug disappeared without a trace. It was reported that on the night before his disappearance he had spoken on the phone with one of the key Egyptians connected to the rocket program and the two men had arranged to meet in Munich the next day. Krug never returned to his office from the rendezvous and, despite an intensive search, was never found. In puzzlement, the West German press offered two possible explanations of the event. Either the Egyptians were angered by the profiteering carried out by Krug, Pilz, and Görcke through "Intra" and Egyptian intelligence had kidnapped the German, or else Israeli intelligence had kidnapped Krug in order to interrogate him and prevent him from serving Nasser further.

Shortly after Krug's disappearance, Wolfgang Pilz had a narrow escape from death. One morning in November, 1962, his secretary was routinely sorting through the scientist's mail when she came upon an air mail envelope bearing the return address of a lawyer in Hamburg. When she opened it, the letter exploded, blinding and seriously injuring her. Pilz was unharmed.

Also in November a package of books addressed to Brigadier General Kamal Azzaz, a member of the Egyptian army rocket team, was detonated when opened and killed five engineers.

Egyptian security men began X-raying all incoming packages and letters, and in this way another parcel of explosives was discovered.

The incidents had their effect on the German scientists in Cairo, who became frightened and resented Egypt's refusal to allow them home leave. Nasser suspected that many of the scientists would refuse to return if allowed a visit home.

The following February an attempt was made on the life of Dr. Hans Kleinwächter, director of a laboratory in the small German border town of Lörrach. Kleinwächter since 1961 had been secretly conducting research on guided missiles for Egypt's war department, and his work was considered an important element in Nasser's rocket program. He was driving home after closing his lab one evening when a stranger stopped his car and made some inquiry. Before he could reply, Kleinwächter related afterwards, the stranger took out a revolver equipped with a silencer and tried to force down the car window. The former Nazi scientist said that he grabbed the end of the gun and began struggling with the man, who fled after a few minutes.

Later the German police found the stranger's car, which had an identification card inside it bearing the name Ali Samir, a captain in the Egyptian counterintelligence organization. Any suspicion that the Egyptians were responsible for the attempted murder of Kleinwächter was dispelled when the illustrated German weekly, Der Stern, came out with an interview with Ali Samir which had taken place in Cairo on February 20, the day that he had supposedly tried to kill the German scientist.

Morale sank among the Germans in Egypt and they began to fear for their lives. Their families in Europe begged them to give up their jobs and return home. The German police and Egyptian intelligence agents cooperating in protecting the scientists were infuriated and vowed to trap the Israelis. They soon had their chance.

At the end of February, in Freiburg, Germany, near the Swiss border, an Israeli agent met with Heidi Görcke, the pretty, blonde, twenty-four-year-old daughter of Paul Görcke, the electronics expert so actively involved in Egypt's guided missile project. The agent, a handsome forty-three-year-old scientist named Dr. Otto Yoklik, told Heidi that he was an acquaintance of her father and until recently had worked for Egypt purchasing equipment for the rocket installation. He asked her to go to Cairo at his expense and beg her father to discontinue his work. He told her to inform her father that an Israeli organization would take measures to prevent the Germans from completing their project and implied that Heidi's father and her family would be endangered if Professor Görcke did not heed his daughter's message. She was given three days in which to consider his request. Yoklik communicated with her at the end of seventy-two hours and suggested a second rendezvous in Basel. He said a member of the Israeli "organization" would be present.

Heidi, who had already informed the German police and Egyptian intelligence of Yoklik's first approach, did not want to meet in Basel, but Yoklik refused to come to Freiburg. Finally the frightened, confused girl consented to a rendezvous in Switzerland.

The Swiss secret police joined the Egyptians and Germans in laying the trap. Heidi, her younger brother Reiner, Yoklik, and a third man were to gather in the dining room of the Three Kings Hotel. Hours earlier Swiss secret service men had replaced the regular waiters, and the outside of the building was surrounded.

Several different accounts of the Three Kings Hotel meeting in March, 1963, have been given. Heidi reported later that Yoklik repeated what he had said at the first meeting— that he, too, had worked for Nasser but realized what the purpose of the research was and decided to abandon the program and devote himself to alerting those who remained in Egypt to the horrible implications of their program.

The man with Yoklik introduced himself as the representative of an Israeli group of concentration camp survivors. His tone was emphatic: "Egypt has undertaken to finish the work of the Third Reich. Your father whether wittingly or unwittingly is helping them in this endeavor. We wish to warn those who in their blindness are aiding the plans of the Egyptian dictator. The men who could catch Eichmann will not hesitate to risk their lives again. But if you can persuade your father to return to Germany, nothing will happen to him."

Heidi said she and her brother listened but refused to commit themselves. They were given another three days to answer and the four parted with handshakes. Heidi and Reiner were accompanied to the border where they were met and escorted home by Freiburg police. Yoklik and the Israeli were arrested that night in Zurich and charged with violating Swiss neutrality and engaging in illegal activity on behalf of a foreign state.

The Israeli identified himself as Yosef Ben-Gal, an employee of the Israeli Ministry of Education. He said he happened to be visiting Switzerland at the time. The news of Ben-Gal and Yoklik's arrest created a sensation in Europe and the Middle East. The German police connected the two Israeli agents with the disappearance of Krug and demanded their extradition. Krug's wife told the newspapers that she knew Yoklik well and that he had even been a guest at her house on one occasion when he had allegedly told her that her husband would soon show up. The Egyptian embassy in Berne took advantage of the publicity surrounding the case to draw attention to the threats made against the lives of the German scientists.

The admission by the Swiss police that they had cooper-

ated with the Germans caused considerable embarrassment
to the Swiss government, which prides itself on strict neutrality. But nowhere was the news to have the impact it
eventually had in Israel.

At first the public was mystified by the arrest. What did it
mean? Who was Ben-Gal? Up to then almost nothing had
been known about the Egyptian missile installations.

But as the story unfolded, people were shocked to learn of
the scope of Nasser's annihilation plan, and the newspapers
were filled with the hideous details of German scientific activity in Egypt. Throughout Israel people hung on every
word or scrap of news from Berne. They speculated wildly
over the true identity of Ben-Gal. One popular assumption
was that he was the German-born husband of a famous Tel
Aviv actress, but to this day his real name is an official
secret.

A few days after the arrest, the afternoon English and
Hebrew news broadcasts of Kol Yisrael, the state radio, were
interrupted with a special bulletin: "The correspondent of
Kol Yisrael in Berne has spoken to Yosef Ben-Gal. He wishes
to convey his regards to his family and tell them he is well."

Even this innocuous communication was enough to stir
the country. The Ben-Gal affair became a *cause célèbre*, and
the whole nation waited tensely for the trial to begin.

Frenzied behind-the-scenes diplomatic activity tried to
head off the trial. Israel suggested to Switzerland that the
best course would be to expel Yoklik and Ben-Gal quietly
and drop the charges since their activities were not directed
against Switzerland. The Israeli press added to Switzerland's
dilemma by pointing out that the two agents could not hon-
estly be charged with violating Swiss neutrality since Israel
had evidence showing the involvement of Swiss citizens and
companies in the Egyptian armament program. This was a
direct violation of the declared Swiss policy of not providing
arms to the Middle East. Furthermore, the admission of the

police and the collusion of Swiss and Egyptian agents also discredited Switzerland's stance. Despite Israel's arguments the Swiss went ahead with the legal proceedings.

Dr. Georges Brunschvig, a prominent Swiss-Jewish attorney, was engaged to defend Ben-Gal, who testified that he was a native of Tel Aviv and had been touring Switzerland when the Israeli Ministry of Education asked him to try to influence Heidi Görcke to stop her father's work. The judges were amazed by the Israeli's fluent German, but Ben-Gal stuck to his story and refused to say more.

The German press, which had adopted a strongly anti-Israeli line in reporting the trial, implied without proof that Israeli agents were running around Europe terrorizing good Germans and sending off exploding packages to Egypt. Previously the same German papers had shown little interest in the ex-Nazi scientists serving Nasser.

Otto Yoklik told the court that while he was employed in Egypt it was his job to obtain cobalt 60 and strontium 90, radioactive materials that would be used in missiles designed to poison Israel's atmosphere. Yoklik presented as evidence invoices and receipts and bills of lading proving that he had made purchases worth millions of dollars. Egypt had purchased millions of dollars worth of cobalt, which had been shipped to Dr. Isis Halil, sister of the Egyptian rocket program's director, Colonel El-Din.

Yoklik quoted Dr. Walter Minder of Berne University to the effect that one cobalt 60 bomb of 156,000 Curies would be enough to poison the atmosphere over Israel, thereby killing all life in the area. Yoklik said that once he realized the true intent of Egyptian research efforts in radioactive missile heads he decided to quit and informed the Egyptian embassies in Bonn and Vienna.

He cited a letter written by General Hussein HaMitzri, a director of the Egyptian armaments industry, to Professor

Pilz wherein a plan to construct rockets with cobalt heads to be launched against Israel was described.

Yoklik's testimony made a strong impression on the court and captured headlines throughout the world. He backed up his revelations with documentary evidence, and cross-examination only served to strengthen further the conviction of his statements. Although it was never actually brought out in court that Otto Yoklik was an Israeli agent, there was little doubt about this point.

Few know the circumstances leading to Yoklik's work on behalf of Israel. He may have been an Israeli agent who was planted in Egypt years earlier, or he may have been what he claimed—a scientist of conscience whose disaffection from Nasser led him to oppose Egypt's missile effort.

Yoklik was born in 1920 in Czechoslovakia and studied at the universities of Brno, Prague, and Breslau. Later he pursued graduate studies at the University of Chicago. During the war he served as a captain in the German Wehrmacht. Of his several published works, the one regarded as most significant is *The Technology of Gamma Rays*, which was published in Lausanne in 1957. In 1953 he settled in Italy where he held high executive posts for several Italian companies and engaged in the manufacture of equipment for radioactivity experiments.

In 1961 he was named director of Italy's Institute of Atomic Physics and Nuclear Technology and also served as an adviser to the Ivory Coast government. In 1962 he worked for a while in Egypt at the invitation of Colonel El-Din who was very impressed with Yoklik's Nazi past and his expertise in gamma rays.

Yoklik denied Heidi's charge that he and Ben-Gal had threatened the pretty German girl. The defendants pointed out that Heidi had herself testified that her father was due to leave Egypt anyway in two months time but was afraid to return to Germany because of what had happened to Hans Krug. Yoklik told the court that they had assured Heidi that nothing would happen to her father or family if Professor Görcke left Egypt and persuaded the other scientists and technicians there to abandon the rocket project.

On the stand Ben-Gal was questioned closely on the discrepancies between his and Heidi's accounts of the hotel meeting. The Israeli firmly maintained that there had been no threats. He admitted, however, that he had told Heidi her father was a "war criminal" because of his work for Egypt and would have to bear the responsibility for his actions.

The presiding judge asked Ben-Gal if in the face of grave danger to Israel he would advocate illegal means to prevent that danger. The Israeli replied that illegal action would be justified if it were the only alternative.

Under cross-examination Heidi more or less confirmed what the defendants said but she still insisted that they had threatened her. She confessed, however, that she had not reported these threats to the Freiburg police and had only mentioned them when taping a special broadcast for Radio Cairo at the urging of several Egyptian agents.

The disclosures by Yoklik of Nasser's armament and Dr. Brunschvig's dramatic summing-up in which he outlined in emotional, vivid terms the Nazi holocaust and the terrible events leading up to the establishment of the Jewish state elicited the sympathy of the judges and the court, and even the prosecutor, Hans Wieland, adopted a lenient tone, saying that he understood Ben-Gal's motives and that although the Israeli had threatened Heidi he had done so for "honorable" reasons. "I find that Ben-Gal did an understandable thing when he wished to act against the German scientists in Egypt," the prosecutor said. "What they are doing there should disturb not only Israel but the whole world, especially since the weapon being discussed has already appeared in public in a Cairo military parade."

He added that the transgression *per se* was insignificant when viewed in the context of what the German scientists were doing in Egypt. The prosecutor seemed to emphasize the high moral implications of Ben-Gal's act. He asked for a symbolic punishment, i.e., three months suspended sentence for Ben-Gal and one hundred days suspended sentence for Yoklik.

The presiding judge, Dr. Heberly, a jurist steeped in the Swiss tradition of neutrality, tried to avoid entering the political aspects of the case but could not avoid it. He drew attention to the terrible deeds of the German scientists revealed during the course of the proceeding. He pointed out that Egypt was mounting a behind-the-scenes offensive that forced Israel to take defensive measures and said that the evil intent of the German scientists in Nasser's employ had been clearly proven and that such activities bring about defensive actions which may not always be lawful. Heberly acceded to the prosecution's recommendation and gave both defendants token suspended sentences. Ben-Gal and Yoklik were released and immediately left Switzerland.

The trial and its disclosure led the Israeli parliament to pass a strongly worded resolution calling on the Bonn government to halt the activities of the West German scientists. Germany eventually responded by appointing a commission to investigate the charges against the scientists. Ironically, the man named to head the commission was Dr. Hans Gloebke, a protégé of the late Konrad Adenauer, who was notorious for his Nazi past. Gloebke had been the chief architect of the infamous Nuremberg Racial Laws issued by Hitler shortly after he rose to power. These were the laws that placed restrictions on employing and inter-marrying with non-Aryans to protect the purity of the Germanic race.

As the result of the startling revelations in the world press indicating the deep involvement of German individuals and companies, Bonn finally passed special legislation enjoining

German citizens from serving Egypt's war machine. The German press relented and eventually conceded that Israel was threatened and had good cause for concern.

The trial had yielded positive results by arousing world opinion and exposing Nasser's diabolical plan. In the face of adverse public opinion, the German and Swiss companies involved in supplying the missile development operation embarked on a more cautious course, and a few firms declared publicly that they would no longer deal in munitions. Professors Pilz and Görcke continued their work, but Dr. Kleinwächter, whose life had been threatened, broke off his connections with Egypt and initiated research on electronic aids for the blind. In Cairo many of the lesser scientists decided that they had had enough. The controversy at home and the constant fear of retaliation, together with the nerve-wearing effect of Egyptian agents watching their every move, convinced them that the large salaries were no longer a great enough incentive. Nasser's program was seriously delayed but not totally disrupted by the loss of many experts. Eventually Görcke quit the rocket development program and returned to Germany in the fall of 1964. Pilz secretly left Cairo in June, 1965.

In Israel the Ben-Gal affair and the publicity given to the Egyptian rocket program led to a full-scale government crisis. Isser Harel, chief of Israeli Central Intelligence, resigned in protest over Ben-Gurion's insistence that the campaign against the German scientists be halted so as not to endanger relations with Bonn. Harel bitterly opposed Ben-Gurion's appeasement policy and his overtures to the "New Germany," a Germany supposedly rid of its Nazi past. The activity of the scientists added force to the arguments of the many Israelis opposing a rapprochement with Germany. For the generation that had lived through the horrors of the Nazi era, Ben-Gurion's *realpolitik* was unacceptable even though Israel needed to trade with Germany and depended on Bonn for a certain measure of military assistance. The crisis engendered by the Ben-Gal–Yoklik trial and Harel's resignation seriously undermined Ben-Gurion's position as the head of the ruling Mapai party. In June, 1963, he relinquished his prime ministership to Levi Eshkol and retired to his modest home in the desert settlement of Sde Boker.

The case of the German scientists in Egypt arose once again in March, 1965, when Cairo's newspapers claimed that Egyptian intelligence had captured the head of an Israeli espionage ring made up entirely of Germans. In Israel the reports were treated as yet another example of Egypt's fantasy press. But the Egyptian government kept pushing the story, dropping hints and tantalizing bits before the usually compliant foreign press corps stationed in the Egyptian capital. Several days after the first announcement Cairo's government-controlled newspapers published the names of the two key alleged Israeli spies—Wolfgang Lotz and his wife, Waltrud, a strikingly voluptuous blonde beauty whom, the Cairo press asserted, had been "supplied" to Lotz by Israeli intelligence.

Egypt's official government spokesmen said the espionage ring headed by Lotz was responsible for sending the exploding packages to the German scientists two years earlier and had also arranged the kidnapping of Krug in Germany. Lotz was identified as a former Wehrmacht officer who had been specially trained in the use of explosive devices and had also taken a special espionage course in France where he learned clandestine radio transmission, cipher, photography, and other skills commonly associated with spies.

The Egyptian claim was that Lotz's assignment was to report on the development of the Egyptian army as well as to frighten the German scientists into leaving Egypt.

The German press played the story for all it was worth. The mass circulation *Bild Zeitung* and the other papers owned by German press baron Axel Springer, as well as the popular magazine *Der Stern,* sent special correspondents to cover the story.

Relations between West Germany and Egypt were strained following the visit of the East German Communist leader, Walter Ulbricht, to Cairo in February, 1965.

The capture of a German who was an Israeli spy was likely to worsen the already strained relations between the two countries.

West German television told millions of viewers that Lotz and his wife were Israeli agents who threatened, pressured, and even carried out sabotage operations in an effort to obstruct the German scientists. Pictures reportedly from the Lotz family album were shown frequently. One popular shot depicted the Lotzes astride two handsome horses indulging in their passion for horseback riding. Another snapshot showed Lotz in the uniform of a Wehrmacht officer during World War II.

At the opening of the trial in May, 1965, the Egyptian prosecutor demanded the death sentence for Wolfgang and Waltrud Lotz. The trial dragged on for months, and finally Lotz confessed to spying on the Egyptian military establishment but continued to deny any connection with the exploding parcels or with threatening German scientists. He told the court—it appeared that he had broken under torture— that he was approached by Israeli intelligence in 1961 in Germany and asked to visit Egypt as a tourist. He consented and upon his return to Germany was trained in espionage work for three months. At first it was suggested that he enter Egypt once again as a journalist, but he countered this with the proposal that he set himself up as a riding instructor and establish a stable and riding school in one of Cairo's suburbs.

The court was shown a small pair of scales in which a tiny transmitter was concealed. The heel of one of Lotz's riding boots was also alleged to contain a miniscule radio device. The ingenuity of this equipment greatly impressed the Arab population of Egypt. The court learned that Lotz presented himself to the German colony of Cairo as a former Nazi officer and soon developed a large following for his equestrian club near the pyramids.

Mrs. Lotz, who had fled from East Germany before she met her husband, denied any connection with her husband's espionage work and made a moving appeal to the court: "I know that our lives are in your hands. Whatever happens to either of us, I want to say that I love my husband now more than ever and I can only hope that some day we will once again be allowed to live in some quiet corner of the world as respected and honest people."

The prosecution relentlessly described details of Lotz's widspread activity in Cairo. It told of finding explosives hidden in his home and of the endless stream of reports and wireless traffic to and from Tel Aviv. It stressed the serious damage the accused spy had done to the country's defense apparatus. But the most dramatic revelation came one morning when the prosecutor startled the court with the announcement that Lotz was not German, but an Israeli who had completely fabricated his Wehrmacht past. He pulled out an unsigned cable that he said he had received from an unidentified source in Germany. According to the cable, Lotz was a German-born Jew who had grown up in Israel and served as an officer in the Israeli army. It later came out that *Der Stern* had uncovered the facts concerning Lotz's background but consented to an Israeli request that the story not be published for fear that it would adversely influence the outcome of the trial. How the true story was leaked to the Egyptian prosecutor is not known.

Wolfgang Lotz was sentenced to life imprisonment and his wife was given a three-year sentence. But Waltrud Lotz's hope of a reprieve was fulfilled, for following the Six-Day War of June, 1967, she and her husband, along with several

Israeli aviators and frogmen, were freed in exchange for the
5,000 Egyptian officers and enlisted men captured during
the fighting in the Sinai Peninsula. Though their return to
Israel has never been officially acknowledged by Israel, several publications have confirmed this fact.

# PART VI

# ❧ Elie Cohen—Spy in Damascus

Until June, 1967, the lush green hills of the Golan Heights formed the frontier between Syria and northern Israel. Here for two decades Syrian forces exploited their strategic advantage atop the Heights by continually harassing the Jewish agricultural settlements clustered in the Jordan Valley near the Sea of Galilee with artillery bombardment.

Now the Golan Heights are one of Israel's major tourist attractions. Almost daily, crowded busses travel up the twisting roads. Below, laid out neatly, are the green irrigated fields of the kibbutzim where until the Six-Day War of June, 1967, brave settlers daily risked their lives to cultivate their crops while asserting Israel's right to this territory. From atop the Heights one can see how vulnerable these settlements were. Syrian tanks and artillery emplacements, surrounded by concrete pill boxes and Soviet-designed networks of reinforced trenches, are now sights to be photographed. Guides relate how on the morning of Friday, June 9, Israeli forces braved the barrage of enemy shelling and stormed the Heights, tanks following bulldozers as a path was cleared. The Syrians were driven out of the area, thus ensuring that all Israeli territory would be safe from enemy long-range artillery.

It is in the Golan Heights that the Jordan River has its sources. The clear, cool springs of the Baniyas, Dan, and

Hatzbani rivers have made the hills and valleys of Golan green and fertile, and Israel, as the holder of riparian rights to the Jordan, sought this same fertility for the southern reaches of the Negev Desert.

To achieve this, more than $400 million was invested in Israel's National Irrigation Project. It consisted of pumping stations which drew water from the Sea of Galilee into which the Jordan and Yarmuk rivers emptied. This water was then fed into a pipeline that stretched from the Galilee to the Negev. The project was conceived on a grand scale since the future growth and development of the nation depended on it.

Israel had tried to solicit the cooperation of her Arab neighbors in devising a regional water plan. The United States, during President Eisenhower's administration, sent a special envoy, Eric Johnston, to the Middle East. He commuted between Jerusalem and the Arab capitals in an effort to reach an agreement on the use of the Jordan waters, but the Arabs were adamant in their refusal to enter into a pact for this purpose and Israel went ahead with its own plan.

To thwart Israel's irrigation program, the Arab League voted to divert the sources of the Jordan River which originated in Arab-held territory. This would deprive Israel of the water she needed for the national pipeline, water that was rightfully hers by international law.

The Arab plan sounded fantastic to Israeli hydraulic engineers. How could they possibly carry out such a grandiose and costly, possibly unfeasible, scheme?

Syria had no need of the Baniyas River, a prime source of the Jordan, but was nevertheless determined that Israel's water project would fail.

In 1964 a Yugoslav engineering company was engaged to construct a channel the length of the Baniyas River and set up a massive diversion installation.

It became clear that Syria was going ahead with the

scheme as teams of foreign hydraulic specialists and dredging equipment began arriving in the country. Israel warned that if Damascus proceeded with the plan it would be regarded as an act of war and appropriate steps would be taken. The diversion scheme was just one of many developments in Syria causing concern to Israel's military leaders. The extremist Baath revolutionary regime under General Amin Al-Hafez boasted of a "new weapon" that would ultimately destroy the "Zionist" state. Along Israel's northern borders Syrian units and El Fatah terrorists—young Palestinian Arabs—launched an intensified wave of provocations. Kibbutzim were attacked, their fields and crops burned. Terrorists infiltrated Israel's border areas and attempted to blow up pumping stations and other civilian installations.

The emphasis on increased guerrilla activity, similar to that of Algeria's FLN movement and Vietnam's Vietcong, indicated that Syria, although unprepared to engage Israel in an all-out confrontation, was ready to sponsor a drawn-out guerrilla campaign until such time as the regular Arab forces were ready for a joint attack. Syria's aggressive belligerence coincided with the arrival of Soviet military assistance teams and a constant supply of Russian weaponry. Israel's defense planners urgently needed reliable intelligence on the scope of the water diversion project—engineering plans, diagrams, maps, and other data—and up-to-the-minute assessments of Soviet influence in the Syrian capital, as well as detailed information on plans for the modernization, equipping, and retraining of Syrian forces.

During 1964 a forty-year-old Syrian businessman named Kamal Amin Tabas often visited the Golan Heights bordering on Israel. Tabas was a close friend of several Syrian army officers and was known to be on intimate terms with General Al-Hafez and other leaders of the Baath regime. Ordinarily the frontier region was off limits to civilians, but Tabas had no trouble in gaining access to the area. He often toured with his camera while in the company of the officer. They would visit the various Syrian army officers' clubs where Tabas was a welcome guest. The bored officers were pleased to learn the latest news and gossip from Damascus, and Tabas was known to be a favorite of the capital's inner ruling circle. His great charm, ready wit, and reputation for generous and lavish hospitality impressed all who met him, and there was even talk that he was in line for a cabinet post. The officers spoke freely of their assignments and duties in their visitor's presence, showed him plans and maps, and reported on the progress of the diversion project.

What none of the Syrians knew, of course, was that upon his return from each trip to the border region, Tabas would summarize his findings and then encode a message, which at a fixed hour he transmitted to Israeli intelligence head-quarters in Tel Aviv. The transmitter was concealed in the ceiling of the bedroom in his elegant apartment in the exclu-sive Abu Romana quarter of Damascus, across the street from Syrian army headquarters. The special radio equip-ment that Tabas had smuggled into the country two years earlier, in the beginning of 1962, enabled him both to trans-mit and to receive messages. Daily he was given orders re-garding Israel's intelligence requirements. The quantity and accuracy of the information he provided astounded his superiors. The mission of Kamal Amin Tabas was probably one of the most successful in the entire history of Middle Eastern espionage, and Tabas, whose real name was Elie Cohen, has already earned the title "Israel's Greatest Spy." His courage, daring, and resourcefulness have made him a legend.

The key to Cohen's success was his friendship with the Baath leaders. He had arrived in Damascus in February, 1962, posing as a businessman who had given up a profit-able import-export enterprise in Buenos Aires to live in his country of origin. At the outset he let it be known that he was dedicated to strengthening Syria's economy by turning Damascus into an important trade center through import and export operations involving markets in Europe and South America. He was already known as a Baathist thanks to his cultivation of Al-Hafez, the party leader, in 1961 in Buenos Aires, where the General had been military attaché at the Syrian embassy.

During his first year in Damascus, Elie observed closely the political confusion that followed the dissolution of the union with Egypt at the end of 1961. It was clear that the Baath Socialists would eventually stage a *coup d'état,* and Elie wanted to be firmly established when that happened. Meanwhile he slowly and confidently developed ties with Baathist leaders and merchants. The latter were impressed with his ideas for developing foreign trade by exporting the ornate, inlaid furniture known as "Damascus style."

He spent much time in popular cafés listening to political gossip while trying to determine the future course of events, and he kept intelligence headquarters in Tel Aviv supplied with a steady stream of political and military information.

The military intelligence was drawn primarily from Colonels Selim Hatoum and Salah Dali, both important men in the Syrian army with pro-Baathist tendencies. It was as commander of the special commando units stationed outside Damascus that Hatoum was to play a decisive role in the Baathist takeover of March, 1963.

Along with George Saif, who was in charge of the press and radio section of the Ministry of Information, Dali and Hatoum began using Elie's apartment for assignations with various women, including Defense Ministry secretaries, airline hostesses, and Syrian singing stars. Often these three married men would take advantage of the spy's hospitality to hold little orgies at which they would get drunk and talk freely of their work and army plans. Elie, who would feign intoxication, remained sober and listened carefully. The next day the relevant portion of what he had heard was conveyed by radio to Tel Aviv. The colonels and Saif were indebted to their friend for the convenient and discreet arrangement. In the oppressive, puritanical Moslem atmosphere of Damascus the disclosure that any one of these men was carrying on extramarital affairs would seriously compromise their reputations and ruin their careers.

George Saif was particularly fond of Elie Cohen and often invited him to the Ministry of Information. The spy was quick to accept these invitations and flattered Saif by telling him how fascinated he was by journalism. The complete trust Cohen enjoyed among his unwitting informants is illustrated by the following incident, which might have had serious consequences for the Israeli agent.

One day Cohen was sitting in Saif's office reading a classified document while the Syrian was on the phone. One of the ministry's directors entered the room unannounced.

"How is it that you dare allow a stranger to read a classified document?" he angrily asked Saif.

Saif calmly replied, "There's nothing to be concerned about. He's a trusted friend."

The director probably had no suspicion that Cohen might be a spy, but the proper procedure in a government office prohibited an official from giving access to classified materials to an unauthorized person. As a result of this incident, Saif advised his friend to lessen his visits to the ministry and to exercise a little more discretion. But nothing changed in the relations between the two men. In fact, in 1963, at Saif's suggestion, Cohen began broadcasting a weekly propaganda program beamed to the Syrian émigré colony in South America. Elie Cohen in the guise of Kamal Amin Tabas would urge "our faraway Arab brothers" to support the Baath revolutionary party and its program for Syria.

By the time of the Baath takeover in 1963, Elie Cohen was at the peak of his career as Israel's spy in Damascus.

He had firmly entrenched himself in Syrian society and was succeeding beyond the most favorable expectations of Israeli intelligence.

The engaging patriot known in the Syrian capital as Kamal Amin Tabas was actually born in Alexandria, Egypt, in 1924. He received a traditional Jewish education and from an early age displayed a strong identification with the Jewish people and the Zionist movement. When members of his family emigrated to Israel in 1949 and 1950, he stayed on in Cairo and served Israeli intelligence. In 1954, Cohen was arrested by Egyptian security agents and imprisoned for two years after participating in an abortive Israeli plot to worsen relations between the United States and Nasser by blowing up American buildings in the Egyptian capital.

After his arrival in Israel he was recruited in 1960 by Israel's secret services and trained as an espionage agent. It was decided to plant him in Damascus, and he underwent an intensive orientation program to accustom him to the cover that had been selected for him. Given the advantage of fluent Arabic and an oriental appearance, Elie Cohen was close to perfect raw material and proved to be an exceptional student.

He was highly intelligent, had great powers of observation, possessed considerable courage, and was selflessly dedicated to Israel's survival and well-being. He felt deeply the historical sufferings of his people and was determined that Israel would be a secure homeland for the Jews.

He was drilled in his new identity: Kamal Amin Tabas, born in Beirut, Lebanon, in 1930 to Amin and Saida Tabas, Syrian immigrants who had been forced to leave their native country because of economic difficulty. Kamal had never known Syria but had been imbued with a patriotic feeling by his parents who retained Syrian citizenship and always spoke of returning—"as soon as things got better." When Kamal was three the family emigrated to Alexandria, Egypt, where his father struggled with a small textile business. (Elie had grown up in Alexandria and knew the city well. He could easily answer any questions about that city; as far as Beirut was concerned, he would say, if questioned, that he remembered nothing since he had left there at age three.) In 1947, according to Cohen's cover biography, the Tabas family moved to Argentina where an uncle sponsored them. Kamal's parents died after trying unsuccessfully to set up a textile business in Buenos Aires. Kamal moved in with his uncle and began working in a travel agency. From there he entered the import-export business and began to prosper. It was as a successful importer-exporter that Kamal would launch the first phase of his mission—infiltrating Buenos Aires' Syrian expatriate community.

In January, 1961, Elie said goodbye to his wife Nadia and their two infant children in Tel Aviv and said that he had to travel abroad for an extended period. All his wife knew was that Elie worked in some capacity for Israel's defense establishment. In Munich, Elie was met by his contact and given a complete outfit of clothing made in Argentina.

He arrived in Buenos Aires in February, 1961, and set to finding an apartment and learning Spanish. After a short time he was ready to make his entry into the city's Arab community and began frequenting Syrian clubs and coffee houses.

He soon attracted attention by the same qualities he later displayed in Damascus. He often told his Syrian friends of the need to institute revolutionary changes in Syria so that progress and advancement could come to their homeland and the rest of the Arab world. Elie was accepted by several influential members of the Syrian colony and was often invited to cocktail parties and diplomatic receptions. It was at one of these parties that he met and favorably impressed General Amin Al-Hafez, the man destined to lead the Baath take-over in March, 1963, and emerge as president of Syria.

In planning Cohen's mission, Israeli intelligence had relied on its appraisal of the internal Syrian political situation. This appraisal foresaw that the unhappy union with Egypt would soon come to an end and that a *coup d'état* by the Baath Socialist party, whose ideology was a mixture of socialist ideas and Arab nationalism, would come to pass. Israeli intelligence hoped that, by befriending the future Baath activists, Elie Cohen would then be able to establish himself in Damascus as an important supporter of the party. The assessment proved correct.

Once he felt that his presence had been well established in Buenos Aires, Elie let it be known that he was planning to return to Syria in order to develop that country's foreign trade. All during this period Elie worked hard at mastering the Syrian-Arabic dialect, which was somewhat different from his native Egyptian accent. He also read everything available on Syrian politics.

Shortly before his departure from Argentina, he called on his friends in Buenos Aires and received letters of recommendation and introductions to relatives in Damascus.

Elie Cohen was now ready for the second phase of his mission.

He left Argentina at the close of 1961 and by a circuitous route via Europe returned to Tel Aviv for further briefing and training. Israeli intelligence felt that it would be best for him to enter Syria as quietly as possible and delay declaring himself openly as a Baath supporter until he was sure that the party was in ascendancy. As one of his superiors grimly suggested, "If you're going to be shot, better as an Israeli spy than as a Baath supporter."

Cohen was also given advanced instruction in code, clandestine broadcasting, and smuggling out secret documents.

In February, 1962, Elie once again parted from his family

and flew to Switzerland. From there he traveled to Genoa and boarded a ship for Beirut. He crossed the Lebanon-Syrian border together with Sheikh Magid El Ard, a wealthy Syrian landowner whom he had met on the boat. The Sheikh was friendly with the chief of the Syrian border patrol, and the Israeli spy was able to enter without having his baggage checked. Ingeniously concealed inside one of his suitcases was a tiny transmitter and other espionage equipment.

During his three years in Damascus, Elie returned three times to Tel Aviv for intensive de-briefing sessions and visits with his family. Each time he prepared full reports supplementing the already extensive and detailed information he had radioed or smuggled to Israel concealed in backgammon tables that had been sent to a contact in Germany and then forwarded to Tel Aviv.

Elie usually prepared for the visits to Israel by letting his friends in Damascus know he was planning a business trip to Europe or South America. He would then fly to Switzerland and stay there a few days. When satisfied that he was not being followed, Elie would fly on to Munich where his contact would meet him and arrange for him to travel to Tel Aviv or Buenos Aires, depending on what the plan at the particular time called for.

In the summer of 1963, a few months after the Baath takeover, it was clear that the revolutionary party was adopting an increasingly more belligerent line toward Israel. Cohen reported on the far-reaching political developments and the changes taking place in the army's command. It was decided that the time had come for his second visit to Tel Aviv. Elie suggested to his friends that it would be a good idea for him to visit Argentina to renew contacts with the Syrian community in order to rally support for the Baath and to study the situation in Buenos Aires so that his propaganda broadcasts would be more effective. He said he was planning to invite several rich Syrian businessmen to set up an export fund for the purpose of encouraging the marketing abroad of Syrian products. He also indicated his intention of initiating a Baath fund and told his friends in Damascus he would seek large contributions from their brothers in South America.

Upon his arrival in Tel Aviv, Cohen held long discussions with his superiors at intelligence headquarters. He was told that, on the basis of the amount and quality of intelligence he had managed to report to Israel, he was considered the country's most outstanding agent and that there was, therefore, a strong temptation to add more objectives to his mission, objectives that would endanger him even more than his previous work had. At the same time his superiors were concerned that Cohen might be exposed. He was far too valuable an agent to risk by overextending the scope of his operations. It was left to Elie to tell them whether their demands could be met without excessive risk.

Cohen was confident that he could undertake anything they asked of him. He stressed that his position in Damascus was secure and there was no cause to be worried about his personal safety. "Isn't this the second time I've returned to Israel by way of Europe with no trouble?" he proudly asked his superiors in an effort to assuage their doubts.

Before leaving for Buenos Aires at the end of his second visit, Cohen was summoned for his last briefing at intelligence headquarters. He was asked to obtain information regarding two major developments:

1. There were indications that Syria was about to receive from the Soviet Union a new arms shipment that would include models of MIG-21 fighter planes. The "21" was superior to the MIG-19 that the Syrian air force had been using to patrol Israel's borders. The Syrian navy was also

expected to receive torpedoes armed with Komar missile heads. These would be similar to the type of torpedoes already in the possession of Egypt's naval forces.

2. It appeared that Syria's water plan to divert the sources of the Jordan River was reaching the operative stage. It was imperative that Cohen find out everything possible about this project, as its completion would be disastrous to Israel's national irrigation program.

Elie left Tel Aviv for Europe and from there continued to Buenos Aires where he was welcomed by his expatriate acquaintances. He had been authorized by Tel Aviv headquarters to draw $10,000 from funds available in South America in case his Baath fund-raising appeal failed. But his many talents included fund-raising, and Israel's most distinguished espionage agent collected no less than $9,000 among the Syrians in the Argentine capital—not an unusually large sum, but enough to prove his good intentions toward the Baath party to his friends in Damascus.

To the $9,000, Elie added another thousand to round out the sum. He then deposited $10,000 in the Baath account at a Buenos Aires bank. With another $1,000 of Israeli taxpayers' money he purchased a handsome fur jacket for General Al-Hafez' wife. Such a gift coming from a wealthy, patriotic merchant was an accepted form of tribute in the Arab Middle East.

While in Buenos Aires, Elie also met with several merchants and encouraged them to import Syrian goods. He advised them to use his name when dealing with Syria's Foreign Trade Ministry, telling them that this would help them in negotiations. In this way he sought to manufacture additional proof that he had worked in Syria's behalf during his visit to South America.

Returning to Damascus in the fall of 1963, Elie Cohen embarked on the most ambitious and active phase of his espionage career. He concentrated on the water diversion

project and was able to collect enough informatio[
questions that were of great concern to Israel:
the exact nature of the Syrian water diversion/
when was it scheduled to go into operation?

Israel knew that Syria was about to intensify its efforts
to complete the project. In the beginning of 1964 the Arab
summit in Cairo had decided to press ahead with plans
for cutting off the Jordan River from Israel, whose irrigation
pipeline was already close to completion.

Cohen's two most reliable sources of information were
his close friends Colonels Hatoum and Dali. They knew
everything about the diversion scheme, and early in 1964,
Cohen was able to radio Tel Aviv that the channel was being
dug along the entire length of the Syrian heights to receive
the diverted flow of the Baniyas River—one of the Jordan's
major sources—and empty it into Jordanian territory. But
the general plan did not satisfy Cohen, and he was able to
arrange to speak to the Lebanese engineer in charge of the
diversion channel excavation. One night, while having dinner with Hatoum and the engineer, whose name was
Michel Saab, the spy learned exact details of the topo-
graphical features in the area of the diversion channel. In
other discussions with contractors Cohen uncovered other
details, and gradually Tel Aviv was provided with a dia-
gram of the Baniyas diversion channel, the time estimated
for the work to be completed—eighteen months—and plans
for the construction of a large pumping station on the
banks of the Baniyas that would transfer the water to the
channel.

This intelligence enabled the Israeli army to plot the
strategy necessary to hamper seriously the Syrians' progress. In several retaliation attacks following Syrian shelling
of Jewish border settlements, Israeli forces were able to fire
accurately at the diversion installations and bring all operations to a standstill. When the Syrians attempted to resume

digging after an interval of a few months, Israeli artillery once again unerringly struck the bulldozers and derricks and obliterated the complete portions of the canal. Thanks to Elie Cohen, Jerusalem succeeded in removing the threat of a water stoppage while avoiding a large-scale war and heavy losses.

During his visits to the border area in 1964, Cohen made a special point of studying the fortifications constructed by the Syrian army along the frontier. He subsequently relayed to Israel a detailed plan of the concrete emplacements protecting Soviet long-range artillery. He also smuggled out his own drawing of the intricate trenchwork ribbing the area. Hatoum and Dali unwittingly provided their friend with a full list of Soviet arms shipments. In this way Israel knew immediately that two hundred T-54 Russian tanks were to be stationed among the hills in the border region. Cohen also sent Tel Aviv photographs of the MIG-21 model that Syria was receiving from the Soviet Union.

Finally the agent was able to inform his superiors at intelligence headquarters in Tel Aviv that in case of war with Israel the Syrian military plan was to attack with tanks and armored vehicles in the upper Galilee and to attempt to cut this region off from the rest of the country.

Another development Cohen reported on—one that was to become a precipitating factor in the Six-Day War—was the setting up of El Fatah Palestinian commando bands under the direction of Syrian army intelligence chief, Colonel Ahmed Suidany, who was later to become Syrian chief of staff.

These terrorists stationed near the Israeli border were destined to become a major threat to Israel's security both before and after the Six-Day War. During 1964 they carried out several espionage infiltration forays with the ultimate aim of thwarting Israel's irrigation program by destroying pumping stations. Though they failed in their objective, they did commit many acts of violence on Israeli territory and greatly increased tension in the border area. The terrorists were recruited from among Palestinian refugees as well as Syrian and Jordanian youth. Many of the commandos underwent guerrilla training in Algeria.

In November, 1964, Elie Cohen made his last visit to Israel and was pleased to meet a third child, his son Shaul, born during his absence. After a few weeks of consultations he returned once again to Damascus.

On a Thursday morning in the middle of January, 1965, he had just completed his transmission to Tel Aviv when he heard loud knocking on the outside door of his apartment. Within seconds ten men armed with revolvers burst into his bedroom. The leader of the group, Colonel Suidany, could barely control himself. "We have caught you at last, you treacherous spy," he screamed at Cohen, who remained calm and simply said when asked his true identity, "Kamal Amin Tabas, an immigrant from Argentina."

Cohen was silent in the face of Suidany's questions, and it is probable that the head of Syrian intelligence thought at first that the spy was indeed a traitor and did not suspect that he was a Jew.

It is not known exactly how Cohen was discovered. The most likely explanation is that his transmissions were detected with the help of Soviet monitoring equipment. Perhaps the Israeli agent had been careless in adopting appropriate security measures such as changing his frequency and hours of transmission. The proximity of his transmitter to the headquarters of the Syrian general staff probably caused interference, and since the private transmitters belonging to the various embassies in Damascus were charted, it is conceivable that efforts were made to locate the mystery transmitter. Elie paid no attention to frequent electrical power failures in the Syrian capital, and his battery-powered transmissions during these black-outs no doubt aided the monitoring process.

Suidany's men thoroughly searched the spy's apartment and found his camera, a reserve transmitter, and other incriminating evidence. Suidany, who was a political enemy of Colonels Hatoum and Dali, sought to use the Cohen case as a means of discrediting these men who had been so close to the Israeli agent. But Elie refused to talk, perhaps thinking that certain key figures in the Syrian government would be anxious to suppress the affair because of the spy's close connections with many key members of the regime. Suidany interrogated Elie for hours in an effort to find out who his accomplices were and whether or not he was operating as part of an espionage ring.

Cohen was forced to transmit a false message to Tel Aviv, but by doing so at a slightly different speed than usual he was able to announce his capture to his superiors. The slight deviation from the usual technique was a prearranged signal to indicate capture. Suidany, who did not realize this, thought that he would trap Israeli intelligence into making revealing disclosures. Tel Aviv decided to play for a time. Syria was not likely to kill Cohen as long as he appeared useful. The next day Tel Aviv replied: "Yesterday's message unclear. Please repeat."

Suidany was satisfied. He thought he was tricking Israel, but General Al-Hafez was impatient with playing games. Once he recovered from the shock of Tabas' capture, the Syrian president acted quickly. He knew that as soon as the arrest became generally known, a major scandal would threaten his regime. He decided to handle the prisoner's interrogation himself.

The disclosure that an Israeli spy had been captured in Damascus was welcome fuel for the fiery invective of the anti-Baath Arab press. The governments of Jordan, Lebanon, Egypt, and Iraq were quick to condemn the Baathist regime of Syria and slander Al-Hafez. Rumors of corruption and complicity within the Damascus ruling circle swept the Arab capitals.

Al-Hafez summoned Dali and Hatoum and planned a strategy which called for eventually removing Suidany from the case and turning over the handling of the prosecution to the colonels, the men who next to Al-Hafez himself would be most compromised by any revelations made by the Israeli espionage agent.

In an interview with the Lebanese weekly *El Asbua Eb Arabi*, Al-Hafez described his first interrogation of Cohen: "I met Elie Cohen after his arrest by Syrian intelligence. At first we thought we were dealing with an Arab who had been drafted in Argentina by Israeli intelligence for purposes of planting him in Syria. Nevertheless, when I looked in his eyes I had a doubt as to his Arab identity. I then asked him several questions about Islam and he was confused. I asked him to recite the Muslim morning prayer but he stammered and explained that he had left Syria as a small child and had never received a religious upbringing. I then realized that my suspicions were correct and that the man was Jewish. I asked him additional questions but he remained silent.

"This was not the first time in my life that I had interrogated a Jewish spy. In my previous post I had had occasion to interview such prisoners. After my visit to the prison, I urged the interrogators to begin a new line of questioning. The next day the interrogators came to me and informed me that Kamal Amin Tabas was really an Israeli whose name was Elie Cohen. Afterward, I saw Elie Cohen several more times. I offered him cigarettes but he refused. He also did not drink alcoholic beverages. He conducted himself in a very brave and honorable fashion during a most trying experience."

Meanwhile hysteria gripped Damascus. Hundreds of people were arrested and questioned. Al-Hafez even investigated certain foreign embassies whom he felt might be implicated in the activities of Elie Cohen. Sheikh Magid El Ard, who had traveled with Cohen on the ship from Beirut to Damascus, and George Saif, Cohen's friend from the Ministry of Information, were among those arrested.

Despite their machinations, Dali and Hatoum had a difficult time hushing up the case. Many people in Damascus knew of the close connection between them and the accused. The colonels realized that it was essential to silence many people and to see to it that the spy himself did not reveal his dealings with them.

It is not known what tortures Elie Cohen underwent during his weeks of internment in a Syrian military prison. Some Syrian agents tried to elicit information from him which would incriminate certain members of the regime; others warned him to keep quiet. The prisoner underwent weeks of physical agony and was subjected to pressure by opposing factions within the regime.

The trial began on February 27 in a military court consisting of five judges. The president was none other than Colonel Dali, and Hatoum was one of the judges. The other three judges for the most part remained silent. Dali, however, was aggressive. He took upon himself the role of judge, prosecutor, and investigator and conducted the trial with complete disregard of judicial procedures.

Cohen's first request was that he be permitted a lawyer. Dali told him that he didn't need a lawyer since the "imperialist" press was defending him. Two prominent French lawyers engaged by the Israeli government and Nadia Cohen tried in vain to see the prisoner.

At the trial, when he was asked to identify himself, he stood erect and answered, "Elie Cohen, Israeli soldier." No foreign correspondents were permitted at the trial, and the only thing known about the proceedings are the segments that were shown on Syrian television. These passages, which were monitored in Israel, illustrated how the Syrian leaders put on a show trial.

At one point Cohen was asked to name his accomplices. He replied that there were none. He was then asked to list the people with whom he had been on close terms during his three years' stay in Syria. He furnished a list of people that did not mention Hatoum, Dali, or President Al-Hafez.

Dali and Hatoum went even further. One day the former asked Cohen if he could identify Hatoum, and Cohen, apparently by previous understanding, said he could not recognize the Colonel in the courtroom.

There was clearly some agreement between Cohen and his prosecutors. Apparently Hatoum and Dali had made a deal: the spy's life in return for his silence. The accused had little reason to trust the colonels but he had no choice.

In an interview Suidany gave to a Lebanese newspaper just before he was removed from the case, he said: "I personally led the interrogation of the prisoner Elie Cohen. I was suspicious of him when I received a list of people who frequently visited his house. Unfortunately I received this information too late. Many of these people were important in the government and in military and economic affairs. One person whose name I cannot mention was one of the most influential people in Damascus.

"I was shocked at the credulousness and naïveté of many important Syrian citizens who were taken in by Cohen's stories, believed that he had vast foreign bank accounts, and accepted gifts from him while giving him classified information."

Israel and nations friendly to her tried everything to rescue Elie Cohen. Leading French lawyers flew to Damascus to seek access to the accused in an effort to ensure a fair trial. It was hopeless. The Syrian government stalled and lied. Appeals were sent by the Pope, kings, heads of government, religious leaders, and international organizations. A well-known French personality, who was not publicly identified, made an offer of tremendous economic aid in return for Elie Cohen's life. The offer was rejected. Israel then offered to release five Syrian spies in return for Cohen, but Damascus rejected this also.

Elie Cohen was unaware of the efforts made on his behalf. Until the end he was not permitted to meet with legal counsel.

In a special interview granted to a correspondent of a Beirut weekly, Cohen was asked among other things if he had realized that he would be hanged if captured. Cohen replied, "I knew I was taking a risk, but like every rational person I, too, hoped that I would have a chance to escape. At any rate, I decided to undertake my mission so as to ensure the future peace and security of my wife and three children. Only for their sake did I agree to this dangerous mission. It is most important to me that they should know that I did not betray Israel."

The trial ended March 19, but sentencing was delayed until May 1 and was not made public until a week after that. Despite the antagonistic tone of the world press toward the Syrian regime because of its refusal to allow Cohen proper defense counsel, even though French attorneys had been promised access to the prisoner, Al-Hafez directed the court to condemn Cohen to death by hanging.

In the Middle Eastern espionage war Israel had never passed the death sentence on a captured Arab agent. This claim had no effect whatever on Al-Hafez.

The public announcement of the sentence said nothing about Elie Cohen's connection with Israel. It simply read: ". . . convicted of infiltrating a restricted military area for the purpose of obtaining secret information that would weaken the security of the state of Syria. For this reason we sentence the accused to death by hanging."

On May 18, Cohen was awakened shortly after midnight and taken to the prison warden's office where the elderly Hacham, or chief rabbi, of Damascus was waiting for him. Colonel Dali arrived at the prison and informed the prisoner that the sentence would be carried out that night.

The Israeli agent was brought to the main square of the city, Margia, also known as "The Martyrs' Place." There thousands had gathered to witness the execution. Accompanied by the rabbi, Cohen was brought to the gallows. As a last request he asked permission to write a letter to his wife and three children. At first he wrote a moving letter in Arabic but then copied it in French so that his last words would not be in his enemy's language.

He handed the letter to Dali and slowly ascended the gallows' steps. The hangman placed the noose around his neck and released the trap door. Within moments Elie Cohen was dead. Colonel Dali wrapped a large white sheet of paper around the corpse. On it was written the notice: "Eliahu Ben Shaul Cohen was sentenced to death in the name of the Arab people of Syria after being found guilty of entering a restricted military area and delivering secret information to the enemy."

The body was left dangling in the square in public view for more than a day, and Syrian television brought the scene to thousands of persons who could not reach "The Martyrs' Place."

Nadia Cohen asked the government of Syria to return her husband's body so that he could be buried in Israel. But this request, as all the others, was refused. In Israel, Elie Cohen's memory has been honored in several ways including the naming of a street after him in Jerusalem, the nation's capital. Now the peaceful Golan Heights, where Russian tanks lie rusting and concrete fortifications are piles of rubble, is a tourist attraction and much of the credit for this turn of events belongs to Israel's silent hero, Elie Cohen.

The uncertainty of political life in Syria was seriously to affect Elie's prosecutors, General Al-Hafez and Colonels Dali and Hatoum. In March, 1966, Hatoum attempted to lead the units under his command in a march on Damascus to thwart a *coup d'état* against Al-Hafez by the leftist, ultra-extremist faction of the Baath party. He failed and fled to Jordan where he worked on behalf of the pan-Arab Baath movement. During the Six-Day War in June, 1967, he volunteered his services to Syria, thinking that his patriotism would cause the ruling powers to forgive him. Without waiting for a reply to his offer, he left for Damascus and was arrested on arrival. After a quick court martial he was executed.

Colonel Dali, who had not managed to flee after the unsuccessful attempt to keep Al-Hafez in power, was tried for treason and sentenced to life imprisonment at hard labor.

General Al-Hafez, the man who had first befriended Elie Cohen at a Syrian embassy party in Buenos Aires, is now in exile in Beirut where he is said to be plotting his return to Syria.

Following the Cohen trial, Ahmed Suidany, the colonel who had arrested the spy and had later been taken off the case by his political rivals, who feared he would succeed in incriminating them, enjoyed a brief period of ascendancy. He prepared the case against Colonel Dali and was later promoted to chief of staff. However, Syria's defeat in the Six-Day War resulted in his removal from that post, and nothing has been heard about him since.

# ❦ The Role of Intelligence

IN MAY, 1967, SOVIET MANEUVERING BROUGHT SYRIA and Egypt into open confrontation with Israel. Nasser, goaded by Syria's Russian-inspired propaganda which charged that he was hiding cowardly behind the U.N. truce supervision troops in the Sinai Peninsula, demanded that these forces be removed. U Thant, to the dismay and puzzlement of most of the world, obeyed, and within five days Egypt had over 1,000 tanks and 100,000 men together with a sizable force of MIG's grouped in the Sinai waiting to attack Israel. Egyptian naval units were deployed near Sharm El Sheikh, the former U.N. desert outpost overlooking the Straits of Tiran, passageway to the Gulf of Aqaba and Israel's port of Eilat. On May 30, Egypt declared a sea blockade.

Nasser, exhilarated by Egypt's folk-frenzy for a final war against Zionists and the surge of popularity his warlike posturing had gained him in the Arab world, was convinced that Israel would avoid a full-scale conflict.

In a secret speech to senior officers delivered the day after the closing of the Straits of Tiran, Nasser said that if Israel decided to break the Gulf of Aqaba blockade, it would be a military action of a limited nature. Then, he added, Egypt would retaliate in full force. The Egyptian leader assumed that if Israel attacked, she would launch the first offensive in the Gaza Strip. It was here that Palestinian terrorist units had resumed their sabotage raids after years of relative calm. Another possibility raised by Nasser was that Israeli forces, within the framework of a limited response, might strike El Arish, the Egyptian stronghold at the northern tip of the Sinai Peninsula.

Nasser's reasoning was that in either event Egypt's front lines would be able to absorb the first assault, cut off Israeli forces, and divert them while other Egyptian units moved up and counterattacked on a massive scale.

The plan called for Egyptian forces, commanded by General Shizali, to join with Jordanian forces in the lower Negev and destroy Eilat. Folowing this, Egyptian air attacks would obliterate Israeli air bases and open the way for an all-out Egyptian air bombardment of Israel.

The Egyptian leader was convinced that his forces, which had been trained for ten years by Soviet advisers and equipped with the most up-to-date Russian matériel, would be capable of prevailing during the first stage and that the conflict would escalate rapidly into total war. He reckoned that in the event things did not go well for Egyptian forces, his Arab allies, the Afro-Asian bloc, and the Soviet Union would bring pressure to bear at the U.N. for a denunciation of Israel, and the fighting would stalemate at a cease-fire. Israeli shipping in the Gulf of Aqaba would be halted, and Egypt would have a territorial link with Jordan, thus completely encircling Israel with Arab troops.

Nasser's faulty appreciation of the situation and his ill-advised early actions were the main causes of Egypt's defeat.

For one thing, Nasser completely underestimated the strength of the Israeli army. As Israel's defense minister, Major General Moshe Dyan, has pointed out, the Egyptian president still thought in terms of the Sinai campaign of 1956 and apparently believed his own propaganda which

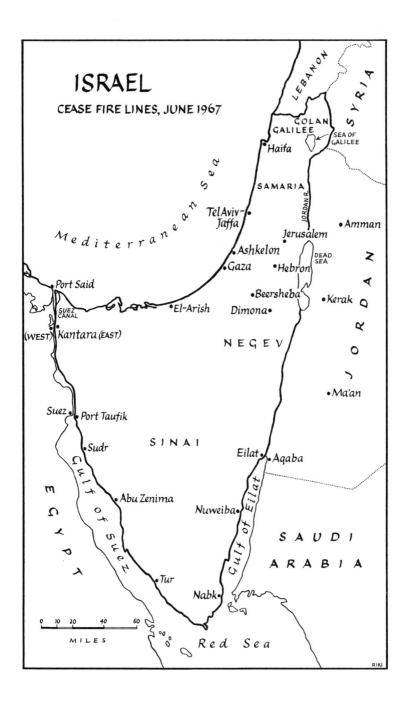

ISRAEL

CEASE FIRE LINES, JUNE 1967

LEBANON

SYRIA

GOLAN
GALILEE

SEA OF
GALILEE

Haifa

Mediterranean Sea

SAMARIA

JORDAN R.

Tel Aviv-
Jaffa

Jerusalem

• Amman

Ashkelon

DEAD
SEA

Gaza

• Hebron

JORDAN

Port Said

• Beersheba

• Kerak

SUEZ
CANAL

El-Arish

Dimona•

(WEST) Kantara (EAST)

N E G E V

• Ma'an

Suez •• Port Taufik

S I N A I

Eilat •• Aqaba

• Sudr

Gulf of Suez

Gulf of Eilat

E G Y P T

• Abu Zenima

Nuweiba •

S A U D I

A R A B I A

• Tur

Nabk •

0  10  20    40      60

MILES

Red Sea

RIKI

claimed that the Egyptian army was defeated then because of Anglo-French intervention and not Israel's military excellence. Accounts of top-level Egyptian military briefings indicate that Nasser was captivated by his own propaganda.

Another crucial mistake was to overestimate the military strength of Egypt and the other Arab nations. Nasser lacked any real idea of how his men would perform under battle conditions, preferring to think that Egypt's seven hundred jets and two thousand heavy tanks promised superiority.

The Egyptians were baffled by the speed of Israel's offensive; they wondered how the armored corps was able to conquer the Sinai Peninsula in four days and how the air force was capable of completely obliterating Egypt's air power in less than three hours.

The failure of Egyptian intelligence was indicated in other striking ways. Most telling was the opening strategy of Egypt, Jordan, Syria, and Iraq. They moved slowly, occupying a position and then relinquishing their strategic advantage. They seemed to be incapable of fully appreciating the importance of a decisive initial blow.

Much has been written about the performance and spirit of the Israel Defense Forces in the June, 1967, conflict: the accomplishments of the air force, the bold strike of the armored corps, the courage and audaciousness of the officers, and the great flexibility displayed by the army. But little has been said about the role of Israeli intelligence which under difficult conditions was able to supply staff officers with up-to-the-minute assessments of the enemy's strength and tactics. The crucial action by Israel—one that made her lightning victory possible—was the destruction of Egypt's air force before it could get off the ground. Israeli army intelligence had pinpointed the exact location of every combat plane at every Egyptian base, both in Sinai and in Egypt proper. But because of security considerations and military censorship, the full story of Israeli intelligence before and during the Six-Day War remains in large measure an untold story.

Perhaps the greatest compliment to Israel's espionage services was paid by a high-ranking Soviet air force officer who visited Cairo shortly after the war in an attempt to determine the reasons for Egypt's defeat. At one point he conceded that even the Soviet intelligence apparatus had not been able to gather as exact and detailed information on the Egyptian army as had Israeli intelligence. Indeed, in recent years the Soviet Union has been sufficiently disturbed over Israeli intelligence to wage a press campaign alleging that Jewish and Zionist organizations act as fronts for Israeli espionage activities. The humanitarian relief agency known as the American Joint Distribution Committee has been repeatedly singled out as a particularly active force in Israeli intelligence-gathering. The Russians used the charge as a pretext to curtail the social services provided by the committee to the needy and remote Jewish communities in Communist eastern Europe.

Even the press of nonhostile nations has contributed to a kind of international mystique concerning Israel's secret service and spying organizations. The well-publicized kidnapping of the Nazi criminal Adolf Eichmann from Argentina and the exploits of Elie Cohen in Damascus have engaged the public's imagination and helped create a super-myth concerning Israeli agents.

The Israeli government is naturally reticent concerning its various intelligence and security agencies. With the exception of the director of military intelligence, the names of the heads of the various agencies are never mentioned in public, and any published accounts of intelligence operations must first undergo censorship lest they jeopardize current activities. Anything in print, therefore, must necessarily concern events several years old and people who are either dead or no longer in sensitive positions.

Israel's leaders began building the intelligence apparatus long before statehood in 1948. Actually the enormous effort invested in defensive espionage began at the end of the First World War. Palestine was under a British mandate, and the small Jewish community was constantly attacked by Arab marauders but thwarted in self-defense efforts by the British mandate authorities.

The tiny defense forces of the Yishuv, or Jewish community, primarily the Haganah, established an intelligence branch called "SHI" (the Hebrew letters standing for the words "intelligence service"). Inasmuch as the Haganah was an underground organization, SHI had ample opportunity to develop secret operational systems. The experience obtained during the pre-statehood period was of inestimable value during the Israeli War of Independence in 1948, when a knowledge of Arab strategy and planning was crucial. With the advent of the independent state of Israel and the establishment of the Israel Defense Forces—the national army comprising the Haganah and other underground groups—the original SHI organization served as the nucleus of the new intelligence apparatus. The best minds of the Yishuv contributed to the formation of effective security, espionage, and counterespionage services. To a larger extent, the special nature of Israel's intelligence services was determined by the unique condition of Israel—a small nation surrounded by hostile Arab states bent on her destruction. For Israel a superior intelligence organization was a substitute for the natural strategic advantages the country lacked.

Because of the close connection between the Soviet Eastern bloc and the Arab world, Israel was forced to extend her counterespionage activities beyond the Middle East and found it necessary to keep a close watch on Communist intelligence activities directed against her. Much of the Soviet-sponsored spying was carried out by military attachés and other diplomats under cover of diplomatic immunity. Soviet agents displayed an interest in almost every aspect of Israeli life—military, political, social, and scientific. On the basis of evidence of Russian spying, Israel became convinced that she had become a major base of Soviet espionage, and this fact added to her determination to wage "the silent war" with every resource at her disposal.

Israel's intelligence, security, and espionage operations are divided among five agencies, each responsible for a specific sphere of activity:

1. *The Central Intelligence and Security Agency* is the major arm of overseas intelligence operations. The name of this agency's director is never made public, and details of its operations are classified as top secret.

2. *Military Intelligence* is the branch of the Israel Defense Forces that collects, sifts, and analyzes material dealing with Arab military and political developments. The reports of this agency form the basis for both long-range and day-to-day Israeli policy decisions and operational planning. The head of army intelligence is usually a senior army officer holding the rank of brigadier general, and he holds a position of considerable importance on the general staff.

3. *The Security Services or "Shin Bet,"* as it is popularly known, is the secret service, which is roughly similar to the FBI in purpose and scope. Its primary function is to counter espionage activity in Israel, and the proof of its success has been the failure of the Arab countries to plant effective, long-term agents on Israeli territory. Lately, the Shin Bet has been occupied in detecting and thwarting Arab terrorist groups both in Israel proper and in the occupied territories of the West Bank of the Jordan River and the Gaza Strip.

4. *The Research Section of the Foreign Ministry* is involved in intelligence work insofar as it complies and analyzes both published and classified reports of political activity in Arab countries. In this way a complete and up-

to-date picture of the events and trends in the Middle East is maintained.

5. *Special Intelligence Section of the Israel Police* deals with procedural and investigative aspects of internal espionage cases as an adjunct of the Shin Bet.

Though these five agencies work independently of one another, a kind of fluid unity is maintained, and joint action is initiated whenever the need arises. From time to time various department heads meet to discuss and coordinate operations. These sessions arc chaired by the head of the Central Intelligence and Security Agency who is in overall command of all intelligence and counterespionage work. He is directly responsible to the premier. A special committee of the Knesset (parliament) is legally responsible for all intelligence operations but does not directly intervene except in extraordinary circumstances.

As in most countries, the men and women of Israel's intelligence and espionage services are anonymous. What distinguishes them perhaps from their counterparts in other lands is the strength of their dedication and devotion to Israel and the Jewish people. The danger is great and the financial rewards are minimal, and yet Israel is able to recruit agents of the highest caliber who serve knowing that for their small country, seriously outnumbered by her enemies, a skillful agent is equal to a brigade.

All agents are volunteers and are thoroughly investigated before being accepted for a trial period. Native-born Israelis are preferred because it is felt that those who have grown up and been educated in the country have absorbed the values and aims of the Jewish state and are thoroughly committed to its survival. Nevertheless, a large number of newcomers have also been accepted by the special agencies. One notable example was Elie Cohen, who had lived in Israel only a few years before embarking on his important and fatal mission in Damascus. In Cohen's case the record of his youthful

Zionist activity in Egypt was a sufficient recommendation.

Most agents receive salaries comparable to middle-echelon government employees. They do not receive special privileges and are not paid extra while on hazardous overseas missions. Rarely are the lives of these anonymous and silent warriors revealed to the public. Most often the veil of obscurity is only lifted at their death, as it was in the case of Elie Cohen.

Several interesting facets of the secret service were revealed when Isser (Halprin) Harel resigned as chief of the Central Intelligence and Security Agency in 1963 as the result of a feud with the then premier, David Ben-Gurion. Harel, who for months after his resignation was referred to in the Israeli press only as "Hamemuneh" (the man in charge), had for ten years functioned in one of Israel's most sensitive positions. The power concentrated in his hands was unprecedented, and his accomplishments were legendary. He was personally responsible for the capture of Adolf Eichmann in Argentina.

Harel was born in Russia and at the age of fifteen joined a Zionist youth group despite the ban on foreign ideologies current in Russia at that time. When the Bolshevik Revolution broke out, he fled to Latvia to escape the wave of pogroms and persecution of the Jews which attended the revolution. In 1929, at the age of sixteen, he arrived in Israel as a young pioneer and joined a kibbutz. Shortly thereafter he became involved in the Haganah. In 1942 he joined the British Palestine police but was expelled from the service after hitting an officer for uttering an anti-Semitic remark. The British blacklisted him—a serious matter in those days as it made it difficult for him to find employment. He returned to his kibbutz and remained there until he was appointed head of Haganah intelligence activities. Those who knew him in the pre-statehood days recall an industrious, intelligent, perceptive man who, despite his lack of formal education, was adept at choosing and commanding able subordinates. Harel earned a reputation as a loyal and considerate chief who would spare no expense or effort in protecting his agents and extricating them from dangerous situations.

His resignation in 1963 was in protest to the handling of the German scientist affair. Ben-Gurion advocated a program of appeasement and rapprochement with West Germany and refused to allow the presence of German rocket experts in Nasser's employ to lead to a showdown with the Bonn government. It is widely felt that Ben-Gurion underestimated reports of the bacteriological and nuclear weapons being perfected by the Germans. His supporters called for a halt in the operations against the scientists for fear that such activities would cause a rupture in relations with West Germany and jeopardize the military assistance Bonn has accorded Israel. As a protest over this policy of appeasement, Harel quit and entered political life so that he could make public his grievances against Ben-Gurion's government. A dominant theme of Harel's frequent speeches was the idealism of the men who had served under him. He felt that calling off the anti-German operations signified ingratitude on the part of the public for whom his men risked their lives without any material reward.

In a newspaper interview a few years ago, Harel was asked if women were used as agents. He replied that women were employed on important missions and often surpassed male operatives. But he was quick to add that he had "strict rules lest the use of women involve immoral conduct." Asked if there was an Israeli Mata Hari, he replied, "Definitely not. Sex was not employed in our ranks to achieve objectives. Still there were women who undertook dangerous missions and completed them with bravery, intelligence, daring, and moral courage." Perhaps Harel's reply seems unduly puritanical but it characterizes the attitude of Israel's intelligence officers.

When Israel Baer, an important adviser to the Ben-Gurion government and a ranking army officer, was caught in 1961 and exposed as a Soviet spy, Harel pointed out that the Russians had even more harmful agents in Israel despite Baer's wide knowledge of miltary matters and his work in important armament research.

On the subject of Communist agents, Harel is nowadays less guarded than in the past. He recently estimated that most of the personnel of Communist diplomatic missions in Israel are engaged either directly or indirectly in espionage activities. Some provide technical assistance to agents and help recruit new operatives. Other embassy and consulate workers engage in cover-up work—obscuring the trails of agents and helping them escape from Israeli authorities once they are detected.

Isser Harel has said that the Communist intelligence services give their spies instructions as detailed as those that Arab agents receive, thus indicating the extent of Communist interest in Israel. Communist agents are paid well, according to the former Israeli intelligence chief, and sometimes Jewish immigrants from Communist countries are forced to spy because they fear reprisals against their relatives left behind if they refuse.

Harel concurs wholeheartedly with the international prestige of Israel's intelligence apparatus and often says with paternalistic pride, "If intelligence work is a battle of wits, then Israel is second to none in the world."

Another key figure of Israeli intelligence is General Aaron Yariv, chief of military intelligence. A pale, scholarly-looking man of forty-six, Yariv is fluent in six languages and has a working knowledge of an additional four. He can speak authoritatively on an amazing number of subjects and impressed scores of foreign correspondents during the Six-Day War with his thorough and witty briefings. Yariv is popular with his men because of his modest manner and outwardly informal approach to the job.

He was born in eastern Europe and emigrated to Palestine at the age of fourteen. After studying agriculture, he joined the British army in 1942. He saw action with a Palestinian brigade in Europe and was discharged at the war's end with the rank of captain. Right after the war Yariv worked with Jewish refugees making their way to Palestine and was also involved in smuggling arms for the Haganah. He commanded a Haganah brigade in 1947 and the following year was named adjutant to the Israel Defense Forces first chief of staff, Yaakov Dori. Yariv later became the first Israeli to study at the French staff officers' war college and was instrumental in setting up a comparable institution in Israel. In 1957 he was appointed military attaché at the Israeli embassy in Washington and was able to observe at first hand the fundamentals of American military planning. Upon his return to Israel he asked for a field assignment and was put in command of the Israeli army's celebrated Golani infantry brigade. He returned to a staff assignment in the early 1960's and in January, 1964, was named chief of Israeli army intelligence by the new chief of staff, General Yitzhak Rabin.

Of his job Yariv once said, "I have never had such a difficult, interesting, or as responsible a position as this." Asked how he bears up under the strain of long hours and constant pressure endemic to his work, Yariv replied, "Intelligence work is like an opium; you can become addicted to it."

Yariv's personal modesty carries over into his life style, and he lives simply and unostentatiously, eschewing the development of any personal power base.

He has been asked many times to comment on the means

and systems Israeli intelligence used at the time of the Six-Day War, but his only comment is: "You can be sure that we used every technique and method possible." More than this he refuses to say, and behind Aaron Yariv's cryptic reply lies the untold story of Israel's silent warriors.